A Critical Perspective: Nelson Mandela- Long Walk to Freedom

DR.NANDKUMAR SURESH SHINDE

ISBN-13: 978-1729649947

ISBN-10: 1729649947

DEDICATION

To my sweetest daughter
Devika Shinde

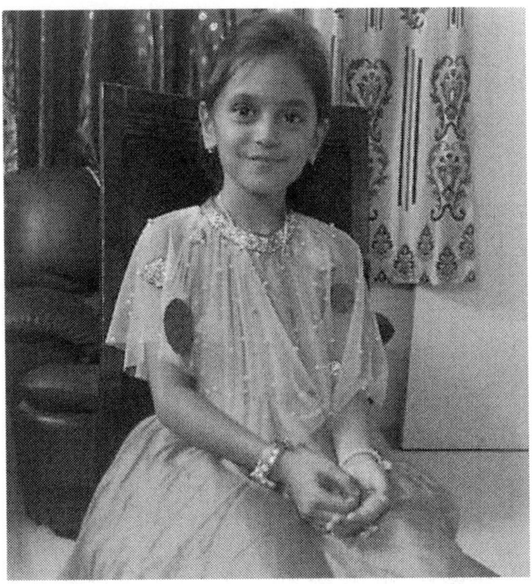

CONTENTS

ACKNOWLEDGMENTS

Nelson Mandela has been an inspiration to all those who want to make change in the unjust order. His highest sacrifice and complete commitment for the freedom of Black Afrikaans will remain in the history as lighthouse for world leaders. His gratitude towards Mahatma Gandhi and his principles make him account as practical follower of Gandhism. He owed lot to Mahatma Gandhi and Indians that's the reason he was honored with highest Indian Civilian award, 'Bharat Ratna'.

Special Thanks to Dr . A.N.Mali for his blessings and guidance….

1 AUTOBIOBRAPHY

Introduction

Nelson Mandela's autobiography fulfills all the distinctive features of this genre. The features can be observed in its content as well as form. The title *'Long Walk to Freedom'* has been reinforced with the subtitle *The Autobiography of Nelson Mandela.* The title clarifies its literary stance and writers inclinations. The autobiography is in the prose form and divided into chapters. It is a narration in a very formal mode from author's birth till the present day. He dedicated the autobiography to his long list of lovable blood clans and he dutifully adds, "To all my comrades, friends and fellow South Africans whom I serve and whose courage, determination and patriotism remain my source of inspiration." Nelson Mandela assimilates his personal family and entire nation South Africa as another family and gratifies his love towards all – love which was the soul principle of his life and duty.

Nelson Mandela completed and published this autobiography at the age of 73 when he became President of South Africa. He selected to narrate his own story which is defined as the 'stand point' in the autobiographical discourse. This 'stand point' which Nelson Mandela chose was very crucial and vital because he wanted to personify his journey from 'rags to riches', from 'literally nothing to becoming everything'. He wanted to write his autobiography when he fulfilled the aim of his life. He could see the life backward from the highest point of his life. As an autobiographer, Nelson Mandela became iconic figure in public life. He felt to share his life story because there was tremendous curiosity amongst all the readers around the world about his experiences and sacrifices. The very act of writing a life down constitutes an attempt on the part of the writer to justify one's life. The every act of autobiography is the judgment of the writer to feel that "life is worth being written down." (Onley 1972: 57). According to Marcus, the critic on this genre adds, "autobiography thus should rather belong to the people of 'lofty' reputation or people who have something of historical importance to say' (Marcus 1984: 31-32).

Nelson Mandela in his acknowledgement clearly says that "I began writing it (autobiography) clandestinely in 1974 during my imprisonment on Robben Island." Apparently Mahatma Gandhi finished his autobiography in his imprisonment time. Solitude seems a necessary requirement for political personalities to write as writing needs time and concentration. 'Want of time' is the main constraint in the life of political figures. Another similar example is the case of Martin Luther King Jr. He attempted to write his autobiography '*Stride towards freedom*' but could not complete it in his short span of life simply because of "want of time'. Martin Luther King Jr's wife completed the dream of her husband by compiling his autobiography. Nelson Mandela admits "since my release, my schedule has been crowded with numerous duties and responsibilities which have left me little free time for writing." (acknowledgement)

The significance of the title

Nelson Mandela's *Long Walk to Freedom* is accumulated into 11 distinctive sections. It symbolizes distinct episodes in his life. His labeling to those life experiences manipulates the importance and his approach towards those events. The style of Nelson Mandela's narration is formal yet sensitive. It takes the reader into confidence and convinces him the real picture of the self. The consistency in narrative style is maintained throughout its length. He gives importance to the direction of achieving the effect on the reader by joining smaller incidents into a unified whole. The adjective in the title "*long*" signifies many connotations attached with the word. It connotes towards the efforts and suffering he endured in his slow 'walk' towards freedom. It implicates his attitude and philosophy towards life. Martin Luther King's planned autobiography which never came into reality was titled as "*Stride towards Freedom*" the title stands opposite to Nelson Mandela's 'walk' towards freedom. The title is more inclusive and convincing. Walking symbolizes hard efforts and patience. Nelson Mandela symbolizes many meaning associated with the word- LONG. The longer size of South Africa as a country is one reason. It is definitely an important implication as it is 25 th largest country in the world. The geographical size makes the country bigger and longer than many other nations of Africa. All the provinces of the country are mingled into the story and the setting involves entire nation, the vast land of South Africa where walking is really difficult. The autobiography depicts the minute details of the land. He describes his native place "Qunu village which was situated in a narrow, grassy valley crisscrossed by clear streams and over looked by green hills." (P -9).

The journey of his life was destined with this land and it accounts for physical distance of the country. His lucid description of his mother land, the different places he had been, and the journey he undertook to visit many countries across the continent magnifies the length of his life journey. Secondly 'Long' also means the historical past and its distance from the present. The colonialism began in South Africa in 1652, followed by the Slavery and Forced Labor Model in 1652, Jan van Reinbeck set up a refreshment location in what is now Cape Town, and requested slaves. The black history of oppression and colonialism has had a "long" and unforgettable memory of every black South Afrikaner.

> "At the end of 1950, there were just four independent nations in Africa—Egypt, Ethiopia, Liberia, and South Africa, which was ruled by a white minority. By the end of 1960, there were 27, with 17 gaining their independence that year alone, as Britain, France, and Belgium all but dismantled their colonial empires in Africa." (The New York Times Upfront, Vol. 142, April 19, 2010).

South Africa struggled a lot than its neighboring countries for its freedom. It's the longest struggle and it symbolizes painful historical memory. "It was during those long and lonely years that my hunger for freedom of my own people became a hunger for the freedom of all people." (P-751). Freedom didn't come easily to South Africa. It didn't come as revolution of a short span of time but it came slowly and very effort fully. In his own words, "I have walked that long road to freedom". He mentioned the long time taken by the colonials to dismantle apartheid. Apartheid was the darkest hour of South Africa but Nelson Mandela didn't seem to tire and relax, he throws new energy into future hope, "I dare not linger, for my long walk is not yet ended."

Nelson Mandela's Legacy of as Humanist Leader

Nelson Mandela is in South Africa what Mahatma Gandhi is in India, a crusader of peace, equality and forbearance. Mahatma Gandhi's autobiography portrays 'the making of Mahatma' a evolutionary change that transformed a mute Mohandas Gandhi into a father of the nation and Mahatma Gandhi. Nelson Mandela's status is as grand and sublime as Mahatma Gandhi's in India and Martin Luther King Jr in USA.

Barack Obama in his tribute to Nelson Mandela on the occasion of his funeral proclaimed his legacy as –

> "Born during World War I, far from the corridors of power, a boy raised herding cattle and tutored by the elders of his Thembu tribe, Madiba would emerge as the last great liberator of the 20th century. Like Gandhi, he would lead a resistance

> movement -- a movement that at its start had little prospect for success. Like Dr. King, he would give potent voice to the claims of the oppressed and the moral necessity of racial justice."1

Nelson Mandela is often compared with Mahatma Gandhi and Martin Luther King Jr. for their common values and stand on certain issues in the betterment of humanism. After his death, Nadine Gordimer, the Nobel Laurate from South Africa wrote: "to have lived one's life at the same time, and in the same natal country, as Nelson Rolihlahla Mandela was guidance and a privilege we South Africans shared". 2 The remarks of Nadine Gordimer was the remarks of White representative who credited Nelson Mandela a joining bridge between blacks and whites of South Africa. Nelson Mandela was a sensitive soul towards his white counterpart and while paying tribute to his favorite writer Nadine Gordimer he said,

> "In his autobiography, he wrote of his time in prison: "I tried to read books about South Africa or by South African writers. I read all the unbanned novels of Nadine Gordimer and learned a great deal about the white liberal sensibility."

His contribution to modern South Africa is beyond counting and his legacy is the vision given to South African government. It follows Nelson Mandela's vision, "when I walked out of prison that was my mission, to liberate the oppressed and the oppressor both. Some say that has now been achieved." (p-751)

Nelson Mandela is one of few statesmen who have achieved almost universal respect not only in his own country but around the world and across the political continuum. His mammoth contribution in dismantling apartheid, his incarceration on Robben Island – where he embodied the struggle of oppressed colored people around the world – and his knack to navigate South Africa through the catastrophe of its rebirth earned him the global reputation of compassionate and benevolent delegate and exemplary peacemaker.

His 27 years of imprisonment for his opposition to apartheid regime, Nelson Mandela victoriously came out of prison in 1990 articulating no resentment towards his oppressors. On the other hand, he defended reconciliation among South Africa's diverged races, advocating the principles of nation-building and co-operative living in peace and harmony. Nelson Mandela's African and international legacy in terms of his efforts and sacrifice to south Africa's liberations struggle his negotiated settlement which laid to non-racial democracy to post independent reconciliation initiatives and conflict resolution efforts at international level. The legacy of Mandela is a mixture of various ideological streams his African national congress – right oriented cartelism, communist thoughts, non-racialism and nonviolence policy of mahatma Gandhi and Christian reconciliation forced the organization to gain public support from liberal democracies, Russia, third world and western Christian countries. Mandela's diplomacy was initially important in winning support for the ANC from South African states in 1960's. After going underground and disappearing out of South Africa, Nelson Mandela visited all African leaders in 1962 and the pan

Africanist Congress(PAN) asserted that the ANC was controlled by white and Indian communist and thus unrepresentative of black south Africans, where not the case. Captured after return to South Africa, Mandela became the iconic hero of resistance to apartheid. His trial was a political symbolism which he attended in traditional African dress in order to bring together African nationalist. His three hours speech from the dependents position justified ANC's political program which established him as an authority leader of South Africa. In prism on Robben Island, he was able to maintain good relationships with PAC leaders and later with activist in the black consciousness moment beside ideological differences. His prison became a laboratory of national politics. He wrote "Here in prison policy differences do not prevent us from presenting a united front against the enemy. This experience can be generalized and applied to our political work outside jail" 1.In prison he prioritized unity among members of anti -apartheid leaders. He also maintained positive relations with the leaders of South Africans black moments though ANC condemned them as supporters of white racism. White government tried to get rid of Nelson Mandela and his stature as the world's most famous political prisoner nullified the possibility of doing so and his ongoing incarnations became the focal point of international pressure on the government. Though he was in the prison, he inspired mass protest in mid-80's which forced the government to declare a state of emergency. These incidents activated the government to officially begin negotiation process.

During the imprisonment Nelson Mandela learned other tribal languages. He made the use of Afrikaans language in the prison. His communication in Afrikaans language made the prison authorities to learn and understand their language. The guards and government officials who were foreigners to the African culture started understanding Afrikaans culture and realized that these people were not savages. Nelson Mandela's attitude was positive and he won many hearts with this attitude. He communicated with reasonableness in his 1989 letter to the state President P.W. Botha speaking of the need to address the demands for majority rule in a unitary state, secondly the concern of white South Africa over this demand as well as insistence of whites on structural guarantees that majority rule will not mean domination of which minority by blacks. He tried to reconsolidate the bond between blacks and whites.

The negotiation for the political mean was the major concern in 1980's between ANC and the national ruling party of South Africa. They were all far better than international mediation of the sort that had the settlement of the conflict in Namibia in 1988. The common interest in the bi-lateral accord was essential. The failure of NP efforts to implement any viable alternative black representatives and the deteriorating economic and demographic trends in the country pushed the government and ANC to start negotiation process, although while retaining capacities for violent coercion.

The ANC leaders and Nelson Mandela had understood that South Africa's capitalist economy meant that an eventual ANC government would need white controlled industry like mining and agricultural sectors. Nationalization of white business would not an ultimate solution. ANC leaders had seen it in the past with the adverse horrible effects of such policies in Zambia, Angola, and Mozambique from having leaved in those countries while in exile.

Contributions to post conflict reconciliation

In this turmoil Nelson Mandela's historic release from prison in 1990 came as an obvious decision. He became an international icon and his popularity in South Africa reached at its peak. In 1994 in its first non-racial elections Nelson Mandela was elected with landslide victory as a first black president. His sacrifice and formidable expertise enabled him to embody the ideal of inter group reconciliation in South Africa and worldwide. Without historical comparison with African whites, the dominant ethnic group in South Africa the new President proclaimed that their language was a true tongue of Africa. In his first state of the nation address as a President, he recited in Afrikaans, Ingrid Jonker's poem about the 1960 massacre of black protesters at Sharpeville. He also saluted Afrikaner fighters of Anglo-Boer war, claiming them as an inspiration for his own post Sharpeville guerrilla initiative among the former adversaries whom Mandela invited to break bread with him. He invited Bessie Verwoerd, widow of the most fervent champion of apartheid and Percy Yutar, a state prosecutor who had once sorted the death penalty against him. His humanitarian aspect was visible as he donated his jerky of Springboks, an historically White's team in 1995 Rugby World Cup . It proved as a touchstone for African Nationalism. President Mandela positively accepted the final report of South Africa's Truth and Reconciliation Commission (TRC) which had been rejected by other ANC leaders as being over critically about human rights violations on the ANC side. President Mandela's legacy is also descriptive in his yielding power voluntarily after completing single term in President's office and exemplified an example for followers.

Contribution to settlement of other conflicts

Personifying a model of integrity and incorruptible of willingness to reconcile with former adversaries, sacrifice of his cause in dismantling an entrenched system of racism and oppression in his own country, Nelson Mandela also initiated settlements of political conflicts in other countries. His Indonesia visit in 1997 Mandela also made a point to visit East Timor's jailed resistant leader Xanana Gusmao and told him that every freedom fighter must remain true to his or her principles, without which he or she ceases to be a freedom fighter, however …without abandoning those same principles, one must remain focused on achieving peace and peace can only be attained through dialogue. Gusmao gratified his efforts of raising the issue at international level and bringing aid to his resolution. Nelson Mandela's efforts in mediating in the peace process of Northern Island and his policy was accepted in Good Friday Agreement a year later. He resolved the deadlock between

Libya and Great Britain condemning those who were responsible for the bombing of PanAm flight 103. His loyalty in adverse International scenario towards Colonial Gadafy of Libya and Cuba's Fidel Castro, was a sign of gratitude who had owed their support to ANC. His efforts in combating AIDS epidemic in South Africa after his surviving son and daughter in law succumbed to the disease. In 1999 during his visit to Israel and Palestine territories, Nelson Mandela told the Israel leaders to completely withdrawal of Gaza Strip and also told Palestinian leaders that Arab leaders must univocally recognize the existence of Israel with secure borders.

Ever since Nelson Mandela became president of South Africa after winning his country's first democratic elections in April 1994, the national anthem had of two songs spliced—not particularly mellifluously—together. One is "Nkosi Sikelel' iAfrika," or "God Bless Africa," sung at black protest rallies during the forty-six years between the rise and fall of apartheid. The other is "Die Stem," ("The Call"), the old white anthem, a celebration of the European settlers' conquest of Africa's southern tip. President Mandela's idea to juxtapose the two, his purpose being to forge from the rival tunes' discordant notes a powerfully symbolic message of national harmony. Not everyone in his party, the African National Congress, was convinced when he first proposed the plan. In fact, the entirety of the ANC's national executive committee initially pushed to scrap "Die Stem" and replace it with "Nkosi Sikelel' " iAfrika." Mandela won the argument by doing what defined his leadership: reconciling generosity with pragmatism, finding common ground between humanity's higher values and the politician's aspiration to power.

But Nelson Mandela's legacy also had setbacks like his belatedly condemnation "the tragic failure of leadership" in Robert Mugabe's regime in Zimbabwe after remaining silent during his Presidency. Nelson Mandela's greatest setback was with his inability to bridge the economical gap between Whites and blacks. When Nelson Mandela procured office in 1994 as a President whites owned about 87% of the land when they constituted only 10% of the population. As a political settlement with the previous apartheid regime, Mandela's party African National Congress, permitted whites to keep their property and belongings. His death year 2014 marked 20 years of democracy in South Africa, and sadly only 10% of the land has changed holders from whites back to blacks.

"Political apartheid may have ended, but economic apartheid lives on. As we pay homage to Mandela on the first anniversary of his death, he should not be deified. He was a man forced to make hard choices, and he left a legacy of both reconciliation and inequality." Says *Bernadette Atuahene, "We Want What's Ours: Learning from South Africa's Land Restitution Program.*

Marian Tupy supports the people who criticize Nelson Mandela for failing to curb the evil deeds which astounded South Africa in the 1990s. In a biting criticism Tupy writes:

> "After all, few have enjoyed Nelson Mandela's saintly reputation while still alive. . . . Those who lived [in South Africa] . . . in the 1990s remember Mandela as a man of peace who strove for reconciliation between the races. But this same Mandela also refused to stop and to condemn atrocities committed in the name of the African National Congress (ANC) against other black organizations — the Inkatha Freedom Party in particular. Thousands of black South Africans died between Mandela's release from jail in 1990 and his assumption of the presidency in 1994. As John Kane-Berman of the South African Institute of Race Relations explains . . . South Africa's descent into a low-scale civil war and the ANC's nonchalant use of increasing violence to obtain political concessions from F.W. De Klerk's government must partly be laid at Mandela's door (Marian, 2010).

Mandela and Gandhi's India

The First South African President Nelson Mandela owed a close link with India through Mahatma Gandhi. Mahatma Gandhi had shown a path of nonviolence and Satyagraha in his struggle against colonial regime in South Africa. Nelson Mandela respected and honored Mahatma Gandhi throughout his life. Media had gone further to call Mahatma Gandhi as "political guru" of President Mandela. India in fact showed its eagerness to honor him with highest civilian award Bharat Ratna in 1990 when he was released from prison. South Africa's adored son Nelson Mandela will be respected equally with Mahatma Gandhi in India. "The Indians influenced our struggle here and especially a man like Mahatma Gandhi. So we respect them, honor them," Mandela said in his speech at the honor of receiving Bharat Ratana. India supported Nelson Mandela's ANC since its independence. In 1946, the then Prime Minister in waiting Jawaharlal Nehru announced that India would boycott South Africa until it abolished apartheid. It was a promise India kept, backing the ANC's demand at the UN and at all international forums. Nelson Mandela too developed a friendship bond with the Indian leadership that resulted in 1990 when he was honored with India's highest civilian honor, the Bharat Ratna.

As South Africa's first black President from 1994 to 1999, Mandela developed close relations with India and the two countries forged bonds over groupings like IBSA and BRICS.

To gratify India he said in the honor receiving ceremony, "We can count today amongst our allies the most powerful countries in the world. We can however not forget for one moment those that stood by us when it was neither fashionable nor easy to do so. Amongst those India takes pride of place."

Second Chapter

A country childhood

Nelson Mandela's autobiography unfolds his mission of life as he says "In life ,every man has twin obligations – obligation to his family, to his parents, to his wife and children and he has an obligation to his people, his community , his country." (P- 748).

Autobiography is the most simple and the best way to understand the person and his deeds. Nelson Mandela's autobiography shows the long journey of freedom fighter and humanist. The first section of autobiography covers the life span of 23 years from his birth 1918 to 1941. The upbringing period or 'coming to an age" is always a crucial period in life. It constitutes the foundation of the autobiographer. Nelson Mandela's childhood speaks about some specific things of his life. It depicts his internal growth and on the other hand his outlook towards the 'cruel' system of racism. The seeds of the protest can be seen at an early age. Like most of the autobiographers Nelson Mandela stared his story from his birth and he associated many historical things along with it.

> "The year of my birth marked the end of the Great War; the outbreak of an influenza epidemic that killed millions throughout the world and the visit of a delegation of the African National Congress to the Versailles peace conference to voice the grievances of the African people of South Africa." (P- 3)

His autobiography shows a common man with extraordinary vision. The autobiography open with the description of his birth place. His birth place is “Mvezo” a place near Qunu a native village of Nelson Mandela. The place where Nelson Mandela’s body was cremated as per his wish. His journey completed its circle in the soil of Qunu, the village Mvezo next to the River. He grew up in Qunu after his father was deposed as the chief of Mvezo. After his retirement, little Nelson returned to Qunu. In the autobiography, he described Qunu as the place where he spent the happiest moments of his childhood. The remains of three of his children were originally buried here, but were exhumed by one of his grandsons, Mandla Mandela. Mandla reburied the remains in Mvezo, the village of which he was chief. On 3 July 2013 the Eastern Cape high court ruled that the remains should be moved back to Qunu. Shortly after this, King Buyelekhaya Dalindyebo relieved Mandla of his duties. On 15 December 2013, Mandela was buried in Qunu following a state funeral, on his family's property in a spot he personally had selected.

His birth place the small tribal village Qunu was cut off from world’s greatest events and “was lived much as it had been for hundreds of years”. Nelson Mandela as a child was blessed with his rich ancestry of chief by both blood and custom as his father was appointed by British as a chief of Thembu tribe. His clan name Madiba, his nick name known throughout the world, was a Xhosa king of Thembu chief in eighteen century. But he says sarcastically that “Although I was a member of the royal household, I was not among the privileged few who were trained for rule.” (p-5). He talks about his father at length and tries to bring out similarities and dis similiarities between both. He was not lucky to have received love of his father for longer time in life. His father died when he was just 9 years old, he narrates briefly about the death of his father " his pipe still lit, he died," (p-17) but he showed his love towards him by saying that "I defined myself through my father" and he adds, " I do not remember experiencing a great grief" yet he certainly felt that my father's passing away "changed my whole life". He proudly compliments his father as "stern in discipline and exceedingly stubborn" and adds humorously that "unfortunately have been passed down from father to son." Father's administrative, leadership skills, mastery over Xhosa history and oratory were the qualities Nelson Mandela mastered later on. He owed a lot to his father who genetically offered some qualities to him. He believed that "nurture rather than nature is the primary moulder of personality."(p-7) His father was rebellious and had stubborn sense of fairness. He had revolted against white Magistrate for the matter of principle and sacrificing the family's 'Chieftainship' and losing fortune and wealth. He sacrificed his honor for self-esteem. Nelson Mandela followed his father's footsteps in the same manner in future.

Nelson Mandela's childhood was marked with his "awareness" about self and the self-assumptions. He was brought up in rustic land far away from cities and cosmopolitan society so the brutality of apartheid was felt comparatively minimal. But his black awareness and self-identity was formed from his childhood experiences in smaller incidents around him. He tried to understand his own culture and pride of being a Xhosa boy. He compares his culture with the whites at many instances. The inferiority complex the identical aspect in Blacks regarding the European white culture was countered in his expressions as a boy. He showed many good customs and rituals followed by his community and restored pride in them. The distinction of bringing up the child between English society and Africans society had the cultural difference. Africans society followed a joint family system and the bonding between the members was deeper and intimate than the secluded relationships of the Westerners. He proudly says, "we do not make the same distinctions among relations praised by whites. We have no half-brothers or half-sisters. My mother's sister is my mother and my uncle's son is my brother." The comparison goes deeper and deeper and he points out the fundamental differences between two cultures. The comparison highlights the bright side of African culture which was called as backward by Western cultural followers. He intended to break the stereotype of African Black .Restoring the pride in his own community he addresses some of the mysterious myths of his tribe. "I discovered the almost mystical attachment that the Xhosa have for cattle, not only as a source of happiness."

Tribe was more important for Nelson Mandela than religion. He was closer to his kinship with Xhosa roots than Christianity as religion. One reason might be that his oppressors were Christian and hence the moral ground for attacks on religious ground was impossible. Secondly Africans were more sensitive towards their cultural heritage which came from their tribal roots. Nelson Mandela narrated his experience as a five years lad, "I discovered the almost mystical attachment that the Xhosa have for cattle not only as a source of food and wealth but as a blessings from god and source of happiness." (P-11) He highlighted his Xhosa identity to counter attacks on Western Christian hegemony and tried to remove the inferiority complex as a black. The Africans were viewed as lesser to westerner in its stereotype but Nelson Mandela shifted the paradigm in calling Africans superior than the Westerners, "Like the people of the East, Africans have a highly developed sense of dignity or what the Chinese call "face". His style of accounting Blacks equal with Whites had a strategy. He wanted to create the wave of self-esteem and pride in the attitudes of the oppressed Blacks. His childhood heroes were typically Africans like Xhosa warriors which he heard from his mother. "My mother would enchant us with Xhosa legends and fables." (P-12) The morals of those fable were his inspirations of morality. He felt that morality was not as academicals discourse but simply the truth of living. In a archetypical tale of a moral order he juxtaposes the myth and reality "virtue and generosity will be rewarded in ways that one cannot know." (P-13)

"My life and that of most Xhosa at the time was shaped by customs, rituals and taboos. This was alpha and omega of our existence and went unquestioned." (P-13) The Mfegu who were outsiders were most advanced and had adopted Christianity and conformed missionaries axiom, "to be Christian was to be civilized and to be civilized to be Christian." P-14.Mandela said that despite the proselytizing of the Mbekela brothers, my father remained aloof from Christianity instead of that his father had deep faith in Qamata, a Xhosa god who was also an unofficial priest. The traditional Xhosa religion was characterized by the "cosmic wholeness" as there was very little distinction between sacred and secular, natural and supernatural. (P-15)

The educational system of the Western style is based more on academic and books but his learning happened through his observations of the true life. His life lessons involved the shaping by customs, rituals and taboos. His books were the tribal living which he was surrounded with, "this was the alpha and omega of our existence and went unquestioned." Though the African life of blacks was tagged to be backward or barbaric but he beautified the old customs and rituals and restored his pride in them. The system based on rituals had it's undefined value like valuing women and ancestors. To respect woman was a contemporary custom of Africans. The belief system was grasped by him as natural knowledge. While condemning the white rituals he says "when I visited the homes of the whites, I often dumbfounded by the number and nature of questions the children asked their parents." Modesty and faith were accounted as a Western values which he challenged by narrating smaller incidents. White people were subject of an awe and fear to him as a child, "they appeared as grand as gods to me."

He came out of that awe and fear and understood that the school system of his time was biased with British customs. The education system was British in its outlook and was full with their customs, their ideas and cultures. The sense of superiority about their institutions and disregard for African culture was the outcome of it. His own name was changed by his school teacher. Teacher gave him new name 'Nelson' as the English school teacher was not able to pronounce his African name. Through the episode of 'circumcision' Nelson Mandela tried to show his belief and pride in his own tradition and customs. "Xhosa people, circumcision represents the formal incorporation of males into society." The custom was old yet he upheld it and justified it in unequivocal faith in the customs of his Xhosa tribe. "As a Xhosa I count my years as a man from the date of my circumcision" (P-30) symbolically the ceremony was followed by the speech of Chief of his clan Meligqili whose word transformed him into a man from a child. He was so impressed by the speech that he admitted that "his words began to work on me." (P-35). His manhood just didn't come with the circumcision but his spiritually awakening from that moment. The speech was a valuable lesson for him, "At that time, I looked white man not as an oppressor but a benefactor" His view was changed and there came a paradigm shift in his thinking about the "white". He realized that the younger community of Xhosa boys were ignorant and helpless and they were "tenants on our own soil." They would go to cities where they would work for in shacks and drink cheap alcohol and live like slaves. They would cough their lungs out deep in the bowels of the white man's mines destroying their health and they had lost their control over their own motherland. Among those young men there were chiefs but they would not rule hereafter as they would have no power to rule. The abilities, intelligence, the promise of these young men would be squandered in their attempt to eke out a living doing the simplest, most mindless chores for the white man. He started to realize the problems of youths and the nation. His meditations on those issues steered Nelson Mandela's attitude towards the reality of his own people and society, community and nation. The words of the Chief echoed in his ears,

> " I well know that Quamata (God) is all seeing and never sleeps , but I have a suspicion that Quamata may in fact be dozing. If this is the case , the sooner I die the better , because then I can meet him and shake him awake and tell him that children of Ngubengcuka, the flower of the Xhosa nation are dying."

Education and learning

As a school boy Mandela faced encounter with the dichotomy between urban and tribal culture. The dress, etiquette, mannerism of both were quite opposite. He was used to tribal mannerism. Clarebury school where he was admitted for schooling had " colonial building" symbolizing western dominium with Africans. It made him realize that "I had to make my way on the basis of my ability, not my heritage." (p-39). The experiences at school were more embarrassing but it "broadened" Mandela's horizons. "I left Clarkbury I was still at heart a Thembu…proud to think and act like one."

Even in his Wesleyan college in Fort Beaufort days Nelson

Mandela attributed his memories of that historical place with British colonialism and Xhosa fighters who martyred their life for African nationalism. His memory capitulated the "steady encroachment of white settlers systematically." The 'dispossession of Xhosa land' and century long conflict by Xhosa warriors like Sandile, Makhanda, and Moqoma, the last two were imprisoned on Robben Island, the place became destined land in Nelson Mandela's life later on. The mission school of the Methodist church with Christian education based on English model, Nelson Mandela was impressed with the English professors and admitted that "we aspired to be 'black Englishmen'" (P-44) . The prejudices were formed, "we were taught and believed that the best ideas were English ideas and the best government was English government and the best men were Englishmen." It was a crucial point in his life to encounter the "western belief". His zoology teacher Frank Lebentlele married to a Xhosa girl, this example began to undermine his parochialism and loosen the hold of tribalism that had imprisoned him. Another example that marked his memory was Reverend Mokitimi's undeterred and bold reply to Dr Wellington who was descendant of Duke of Wellington which created a feeling, " that a black man did not have to defer automatically to a white however senior he was." (P-45) Another incident he reported which left an impression on his mind was "the Xhosa poet Krune Mqhayi's visit" to his college. His appearance in tribal dress accompanied by A White principal left an electrifying effect over him. Mqhayi's poetic illustration and praising the Xhosa legends and myths moved Mandela with intense pride about being

Xhosa. His dual identity one as Xhosa and other as African always floated him throughout his college education.

College of Fort Hare

At his 21st year of age he joined University College of Fort Hare "it was Oxford and Cambridge, Harvard and Yale for me." (P-51) The Christian system exhorted to obey God and respect the political authorities and be grateful for the educational opportunities afforded to the blacks of Africa. These colleges were criticized for being colonist in their attitude and practices but Nelson Mandela conformed his trust in them as , " their benefits outweighed their disadvantages" (P-52) He appreciated the missionary schools on the ground that while morally rigid , they were far more open than the raciest principles underlying government schools. Here Nelson Mandela met Professor Z.K.Matthews who was the greatest scholar of Africa, the very model of intellectual. His journey from a miner's child to the greatest height was an example in front of Black aspirants. There Nelson Mandela played several roles like Bible teacher and theater artist. This helped him to meet great people of African nationalism like Oliver Tambo.

One incident opened Nelson Mandela's eyes about the superiority of whites. His friend Paul straightforwardly offended the white magistrate who ordered Paul to bring him postal stamps. Nelson Mandela couldn't withstood his friend and followed the duty of the white magistrate. The incident gave him new confidence as he said, "I was beginning to realize that a black man did not have to accept the dozens of petty indignities directed at him each day." (P-59)

The first chapter ends on a dramatic note of Mandela's proposed forceful marriage by Regent of his community. Nelson Mandela was asked to get married as per the norm of the community but he protested against the order of Regent and ran away to avoid the marriage. He added humorously, "While I would not have considered fighting the political system of the white man, I was quite prepared to rebel against the social system of my own people." In this way Nelson Mandela's destiny brought him to the city with which his life was tied. "Johannesburg always had been depicted as a city of dreams." (P-69) His journey from childhood to youth was his transformation from a naïve child of Qunu to the self-confident and rebellious Youth of Johannesburg. From darkness to light, from ignorance to knowledge and from safety to hazardous challenges, Nelson Mandela's journey of life reached its perfect stage for new fight. His words speak for itself, "the prospects of Johannesburg was so exciting that I felt as though I slept on a beautiful feather of bed that night."

Chapter Two

Johannesburg

Nelson Mandela's first visit to Johannesburg was not intended but accidental and as a runaway and finding shelter and job. The dreamy imagination vanquished with the dreadful reality of the city as he described "I saw black men in dusty overalls looking tired and bent. They lived on the grounds in bleak, single Rex Barracks that contained hundreds of concrete bunks separated from each other only by inches." His long journey from country yard to metro city was an eye opening and stimulating inwardly. At his first encounter he saw the naked truth about black sufferings, "it was my first sight of South African capitalism at work and I knew I was in for a new kind of education." Mahatma Gandhi's transformation occurred when he travelled through third class train compartments. Nelson Mandela's also witnessed poverty in Johannesburg during his train journey.

After several attempts he got his first job as a night watchman. Johannesburg gave him an access to political environment and politically motivated youths. He started meeting political figures. He started visiting ANC office and his meeting with great politicians and leaders added knowledge and contacts like ANC President general Dr. Xuma. He met Walter Sisulu who became his companion in his struggle throughout his life. His innocent ideas started getting shattered with bitter realities. His had held a belief that proficiency in English and success in business were direct result of high academic achievement which was shattered when he came to know about Walter Sisulu's educational status. He came to know from him that Sisulu had not gone beyond standard VI to school. "It was another lesson from Fort Hare that I had to unlearn in Johannesburg." (P-80)

Mr Sidesky who gave him a job in his firm. There he realized how difficult it was to get even an inferior job. He started to feel the pains of his countrymen and said "only mass education, would free my people arguing that an educated man could not be oppressed because he could think for himself." At a White law firm working as a clerk Nelson Mandela came across the color prejudice. In the office he was given a different cup than the white man's cup. Nelson Mandela refused to accept the tea in that preserved cup for blacks and reported his protest against the prejudice.

His co African black worker Gaur Radebe gave him a lesson that, "a degree was not in itself a guarantee of leadership." (P-85) His informal life training had already begun by facing the bitter situations and experiences. He met his first white friend Nat Bregman who was a member of communist party and preached him the virtues of communism and persuaded him to join the party but Nelson Mandela turned the offer down on the ground that , " I was also quite religious and the party's antipathy to religion put me off." He sought that the communist philosophy was not worth for

South Africa as it was successful in Russia, Germany or England. The problem of South Africa was purely "racial". Nelson Mandela was comprehensively opposite to communism and considered "a foreign ideology unsuited to the African situation." (p-115) He unlearned many unnecessary dogmatism related with education, knowledge and mannerisms. His settling at Alexandra opened up new avenues of learning and experiences which he needed to groom himself for the loner battle against the apartheid. His attendance at ANC meetings marked his involvement in politics and finally he actively started participating in a public rally. His career began as the African Nationalist. He participated in a protest against the fare hike. It was a learning lesson for him. Nelson Mandela realized the value and impact of public boycott, the experience for him was "exhilarating and inspiring" and "after nine days during the buses ran empty, the company reinstated the fare to four pence." (P-100)

It was Johannesburg where Nelson Mandela enticed the self-knowledge and his aim in life became clear with each experience. He started to realize his callings as he said, "having a successful career and a comfortable salary were no longer my ultimate goal." The self-realization happened gradually. "My duty was to my people as a whole, not just particular branch or section." These words directed his path.

The humiliating experiences consolidated his inner spirit for the fight against apartheid. One such incident mentioned in the book was his arrest in a train which was not meant to be boarded by Africans. His mention as "kaffir" stunned him and asserted his goal as "to sacrifice for the cause of the oppressed."(P-106) Alike Mahatma Gandhi he too was humiliated in the train for racism.

Chapter- Three

Birth of a Freedom Fighter

"Change was in the air in the 1940s" (P-110) these lines opened the chapter. Nelson Mandela became ready for bigger and meaningful actions. Walter Sisilu was the leader of the ANC and his house was Mecca for freedom fighters. Lembede, A.P. Mda, Dr.Xuma, Peter Mda, Oliver Timboo were the young leaders who left impressions on Mandela's life and thinking. Youth League was formed in 1943. ANC's fundamental policy differed from Youth League. Youth League was dedicated to African Nationalism and called uniting force for all African Tribes. The Youth league decided to protest against anti African laws of 1913 land act, Urban Areas Act of 1923, Color Bar Act, Native administrative act. The acts were the symbols of unjust. It seemed as the illusion that whites would allow Africans to have control over their own destiny. The Indian communities struggle against the Ghetto act (1946) impressed Nelson Mandela and he found the quality that required to erupt the mass protest of agitations in a peaceful way. "Indian people register an extraordinary protest against color oppression in a way that Africans and ANC had not," He owed his gratification to Indians and the legacy of Mahatma Gandhi,

> "The Indian campaign harkened back to the 1913 passive resistance campaign in which Mahatma Gandhi led a tumultuous procession of Indians crossing illegally from Natal

> to Transvaal. That was history, this campaign was taking place before my own eyes." (P-119)

But he didn't want to go with either communist or Indians because of the threat of getting their movement being high jacked by them "because of their superior education, experience and training." (P-124) In 1947 Mandela was elected to the Executive Committee of the Transvaal ANC as result he became instrumental and important figure in carrying out a "doctor's pact" a joint force Indian Congress, Natal Indian Congress and ANC. The political turmoil of 1948 General Elections which were won by The Nationalist Party led by Dr. Danial Malan whose was a apartheid man which literally means "apartness", the often haphazard segregation of the past three hundred years was to be consolidated into a monolithic system that was diabolical in its detail, inescapable in its reach and overwhelming power. Apartheid and Christian church went hand in hand. The victory of Nationalist party in Mandela's word was like, "Israelites journey to the Promised land….justification of their view that South Africa should be white man's country forever." (P-128) The Nationalist party started imposing more oppressive laws and acts which instigated the ANC to retaliate with new strategies. When the Gandhian way of protest was discussed in the meeting all said, "the time has come for mass actions along the lines of Gandhi's non-violence protest in India …..the ANC leaders , we said, had to be willing to violate the law and if necessary, go to prison for their belief as Gandhi had."(P-130) Nelson Mandela's political camp opposed Dr. Xuma's leadership and defeated him in ANC elections and Dr. Moroka became President of ANC, Walter

Sisulu as Secretary General and Oliver Tamboo as National Executive. On the freedom day strike 1st May witnessed more than two third of African workers participated in the mass call off and stayed at home. In the mass process police open fired and killed eighteen Africans. 26th June had become a landmark day in freedom struggle and observed as "freedom day." Nelson Mandela felt that his opposition to communism and Indian were based on the fact that "indians expoites black labour in their shopkeepers and merchants" (p-142) which Walter disagreed and suggested that Indians, coloreds and Afrikaners were inextricably bound together. The ANC council resolved that ANC would hold demonstrations on 6th April 1952 as a prelude to the launching of the campaign for the Defiance of unjust law. That same day white South Africans would be celebrating the three hundredth anniversary of Jan Van Riebeeck's arrival at the Cape Town in 1652. "We also discussed whether the campaign should follow the Gandhian principles of non-violence or as the Mahatma called 'Satyagraha' a nonviolence that seeks to conquer through conversion." (p-146) but Nelson Mandela was more practical than illogical as he stated, "I saw nonviolence on the Gandhian model not as an inevitable principle but as a tactic to be used as the situation demanded." (P-146) On the first day of the Defiance Champaign more than 250 volunteers around the country violated various unjust laws and were imprisoned. In next five months 8500 people took part that included doctors, lawyers, teachers, factory workers, students, ministers were defied and went to jail. The campaign received an enormous amount of publicity and the membership of the ANC shot up from 20000 to 100000. On 30th July 1952 at the height of Defiance Campaign, Nelson Mandela was arrested on the charge of violation of suppression of communism act and were proven guilty in the court and sent to jail with nine months hard labor imprisonment. It was his first encounter with jail. In the protest he admired the protesters by saying that "there was not a single act of violence on our side." He felt it as a great sense of accomplishment and satisfaction. The campaign made him free from sense of doubt and overwhelmed him with the power of his decisions. His following lines reflected his confidence as a freedom fighter, "I could walk upright like a man and look everyone in the eye with the dignity that comes from not having succumbed to the oppression and fear. I had come of age as a freedom fighter" (P-161)

Part four : The Struggle is my life

Nelson Mandela's became one of the four the Deputy President of ANC under the leadership of Albert Luthuli. Shortly ANC faced a ban on meetings and gatherings by the white government that forced ANC to plan the strategy to be known as the Mandela plan or simply, M-plan. As a part of the plan the ANC introduced an elementary course of political lectures for its members throughout the country. These lectures were not only meant to educate but to hold the organization together. Nelson Mandela fulfilled two duties together his political work in the struggle and earning livelihood as an attorney for his family. He started a law firm named as "Mandela and Tambo" in Johannesburg. The purpose was to provide legal help for desperate and poor blacks, who were charged under the crimes like walking through a white's only door, riding a whites only bus, using whites only drinking fountain or walking whites only bridge. Nelson Mandela and Tambo started to help ordinary Africans. "It was a place where they might actually feel proud to be represented by men of their own skin color. This was a reason I had become a lawyer in the first place." (P-173). He also tragically admitted that no matter how well they pursue their career as attorneys they could never become a prosecutor, a magistrate or a judge. They frequently encountered prejudice in the court itself. Police would address them as "Kaffir lawyer". The judge would overlook them or look suspiciously. The racial harassment was very common in the court but Nelson Mandela flamboyantly encountered these incidents and emerged as an entertainer and justice bearer in the court. He mastered the art of communication. The brutal attitude of the government reached to such level that he condemned the government for its ruthlessness and in more articulated words he said,

> "Non-violence was useless strategy and could never overturn a white minority regime bend on retaining its power at any cost. At the end of the day, I said, violence was only weapon that would destroy apartheid" (P-182)

Nelson Mandela becomes skeptical about Gandhian way to fight against the apartheid,

> "In India, Gandhi had been dealing with foreign power that ultimately was more realistic and far sighted. That was not the case with the Afrikaners in South Africa. Non-violent passive resistance is effective as long as your opposition adheres to the same rule as you do"(P-183).

He believed that a peaceful protest if met with violence, its effectiveness ends there itself. Non-violence was just a moral principle for Nelson Mandela and a strategy but he also believed that there was no moral goodness in using an ineffective weapon. His speeches on his violent methods and means attracted good public support but he realize that such speeches could provoke the enemy to crush the organization entirely as the enemy was stronger than them. He accepted the censure and there after faithfully defended policy of violence in public. "But in my heart, I knew that non-violence was not the answer"(p-184).

With Walter Sisulu, Nelson Mandela made a plan that they should arrange to visit Peoples Republic of China and discuss with them the possibility of supplying weapon for an armed struggle. Mandela's idea was turned down by the ANC but Walter managed to reach China. He came back with encouragement from China but without guns. Nelson Mandela received the banning orders from Government. He had already prepared a presidential address for ANC's Transvaal conference. His speech was read by Andrew Kunene which subsequently became famous as "The no easy walk to freedom" the phrase he borrowed from Jawaharlal Nehru and proclaimed that to take up the operation of South Africa's freedom has been sanctioned by humanity and was the highest aspiration of every freeman. He realized that Governments attitude could not be changed. The lesson he took away from the campaign was that in the end they had no alternative to armed and violent resistance. Over and over again ANC had used all the non-violent weapons but without any substantial success. Such as speeches, deputations threats, marches, strikes and voluntary imprisonment all to no avail for whatever they did was met by an iron hand. As a freedom fighter he learned the hard way that it was the oppressor who defines the nature of the struggle and the oppressor is often left no recourse but to use methods that mirror those of the oppressor,. The chapter ends with these lines, “At a certain point, one can only fight fire with fire”

Chapter-Five

Treason

The "Treason" chapter covered the most turmoil period of Nelson Mandela's struggle in his personal as well as political life. He was arrested on 5th December 1956 in his own house the warrant stated, "High Treason", the arrest embarrassed him as," it is not pleasant to be arrested in front of one's children even though one knows that one is doing right."(P-231) The arrest and trial was a learning experience. It would prepare him for bigger police operations. He stated the comment as, "It is said that no one truly knows a nation until one has been inside its jails." Jail was inevitable destiny in his life.

Turmoil in personal life

His personal life also was on stake due to his political commitments and his marriage with Evelyn had begun to unravel. Their ways were divided and their ends were also moving towards different directions. Mandela's life has become a life of a politician and Evelyn was devoted to religion. "I tried to persuade her of the necessity of the struggle, while she attempted to persuade me of the value of religious faith" (p-240) Nelson Mandela realized that the marriage was no longer tenable and finally they broke away from each other. Nomzamo Winifred Madikizela, the much debated and discussed personality of Mandela's life appeared in his life and within short period of knowing each other Winnie and Nelson Mandela knotted the tie of marriage on 14 th June 1958. Winnie gave him a ray of hope and he felt that he had a new and second chance at life. "My love for her gave me added strength for the struggle that lay ahead." (P-253) His decision of leaving Evelyn and marring Winnie was seen as 'political choice' than 'personal.'

General Election -1958

The major national event proposed in the country in 1958 was the general election, "three million Whites could participate, but none of the thirteen millions Africans" (p-254). ANC's efforts bore fruits as ANC Women's League mobilized the women across the country in both city and rural areas. They reacted with the fury to the state's insistence that they carry passes. The women were courageous, persistent, enthusiastic and indefatigable and their protest that was novel and intense. Winnie too was determined to get arrested despite of her pregnancy and her husband's opposition. Nelson Mandela sympathized with Winnie for her commitment in the struggle though their married life and motherhood both had burdened her heavily. Her struggle was overshadowed by Nelson Mandela's image. He sympathized with her saying, "other's often saw her as "Mandela's wife'. It was undoubtedly difficult for her to form her own identity in my shadow." (P-265) The election was a farce but it went on smoothly under heavy security. The newly elected Government in 1959 parliament passed the promotion of

Bantu Self Government Act. This was the foundation of "grand Apartheid" and the introduction of University Education Act which barred the non-whites from racial 'open' universities. ANC Chief Luthuli put forth ANC's policy in his defense in the court. He asserted that ANC had sincerely strived for racial harmony. He clarified that belief in the innate goodness of man and the moral persuasion plus economical pressure could well lead to a change of heart on the part of white South Africans. In the discussion at ANC meeting the non-violent policy of ANC was strongly criticized by Nelson Mandela. He said, " there was a difference between nonviolence and pacifism. Pacifists refused to defend themselves even when violently attacked but ....nonviolent had to defend themselves when they were attacked." (P-277)

Sharpeville Tragedy a murder of Humanism

The Sharpeville tragedy resembles to India's Jalianwala Bagh massacre. December 1959 ANC annual conference unanimously voted to initiate a massive countrywide anti-pass campaign in the wake of African countries freedom wave. The British Prime Minister Harold Macmillan on his visit to South Africa talked of 'winds of change' sweeping Africa.

Sharpeville was a small township near Johannesburg where thousands of demonstrators were protesting against the pass when police open fired the crowd and killed sixty nine Africans. The massacre rocked the entire South Africa. 28th March was observed as a national day of mourning and protest the atrocities at

Sharpeville and in the city Orlando, Nelson Mandela burned the passes in front of masses and media. Thousands of demonstrators whirled the country and Government declared state emergency. Nelson Mandela was arrested again without warrant and was left to attend the Treason Trial in Pretoria. In the trial three judges rose above their prejudices, their education and their background and Justice Rumpff declared the accused, Nelson Mandela as "not guilty."

The Black Pimpernel

After the verdict of Treason Trial Nelson Mandela's journey of struggle became more intense and difficult as he had come on the gun point of the Government. In secret meeting of ANC National Executive it was decided on Nelson Mandela's suggestion that instead of strike against the government they should "stay at home." Nelson Mandela went underground which he stated in a tragic manner, "to be a black man in South Africa meant not to trust anything, which was not unlike living underground for one's entire life." (p-315) His hideout were literally his invisibility "a seismic psychological shift." Travelling secretly and still attending public meetings at night was a highest risk and he accounted few narrow escapes when Colonel Spengler the Security Chief was in an adjacent car and other incident when two policemen smiled at him and allowed him to escape. Many policemen also showed their loyalty to him and Winnie. The struggle had reached a point of virtual war between state and the liberation movement. The raids were staged on opposition leaders and government declared that those supporting the strike were "playing with the fire." The military exercised its largest call up since war. Tanks, helicopters hovered the land and skies of cities. Police holidays were cancelled and "the stay at home" campaign was threatened by the government. On 29th May the first day of 'stay at home' hundreds of thousands of people risked their jobs and livelihood by not going to work." The white celebration of Republic Day was drowned out by our protest." (P-319) Nelson Mandela talking to different people of political circle affirmed "stay at Home "as a "tremendous success." The attitude of the government made ANC leaders to change their approach and he realized that

> "The days of nonviolence struggle was over If the government reaction is to crush by naked force our nonviolence struggle, we will reconsider our tactics. In my mind we are closing the chapter of non-violence policy." (P-321)

Nelson Mandela became very anxious to change the paradigm towards "armed struggle" His African expression," *Sebatana na se bokwe ka diatla*' (The attacks of the wild beast cannot be averted with only bare hands.) He felt that they had no choice but to turn to violence. On Nelson Mandela's forceful and strong ideology ANC decided to keep military movement as a separate organ but under the control of ANC. But Nelson Mandela was skeptical about the support of Indian colleagues, J.N.Singh echoed "Nonviolence has not failed us…we have failed nonviolence." (P-323) Indian leaders started speaking sorrowful tone about the end of non-violence. But finally there was a resolution and "The congresses authorized me to go ahead and form a new military organization, separate from the ANC." (P-323) Nelson Mandela considered the decision as a 'fateful.' For forty years the ANC had treated non-violence as a core principle beyond a question of debate but now ANC would be a different organization and had embarked on dangerous path- path of organized violence. "*Umkhonto we Sizwe*" (The spear of the nation) or MK was founded with Nelson Mandela as a Chairman. David Motsamayi was the name taken by Nelson Mandela during his hideouts. His secret hidings and meetings were speculating a new conspiracy of violence attack on the government. Winnie brought him an air rifle and he starred practicing the shots at doves. He undertook a mission in African nations to arrange political and economic support for their new military force and training for ANC men. Nelson Mandela viewed that "Military training must go hand in hand with political training, form a revolution is not just a question of pulling a trigger, its purpose is to create a fair and just society." (P-364)

Rivonia

After finishing his secret tour, Nelson Mandela reached South Africa and breathed deeply. The air of one's home always smells sweet after one has been away. His adventurous secret trip to various African countries was extremely successful as he reassured those leaders that ANC would be reshaping the Congress alliance so that ANC would be seen as the leader especially on issues directly affecting Africans. This was a serious proportion and the entire leadership of ANC had to be consulted and as a part of this move. Nelson Mandela should go down to Durban and brief Chief Luthuli. As MK was planning the sabotage and on the way to Pietermaritzburg, Nelson Mandela was arrested and he realized that, "my seventeenth months freedom were about to end". The trial he thought to use not as a test of the law but as a platform for our beliefs. They would not deny that they had been involved in sabotages but would not deny that we had left the non-violence policy at the back.

They decided to disregard the punishment but use trial to strengthening their cause of struggle. They made a strategy to disagree the state's central contention to embark guerrilla warfare but to take it in the failure of sabotage and disclaiming the murders, property damaging and attacks on government stations. They decided to explain Operation Mayibuye to the court to make them believe their plans and fight for the rights. Nelson Mandela's case was week because there were direct evidences against him. Documents were clearly showing his absconding from the country and had arranged military training for the people. The formation of

Umkhonto We Sizwe and his own handwriting of the document named 'how to be good communist' were the clear evidences against him and he felt they were likely to hang no matter what they said so they decided to speak the truth. In his defense Nelson Mandela strongly asserted that his struggle was not under the influence of foreigners or communist. His protest was his own individual spirit for his own people and the influence of his own leaders. He had a right to protest against injustice in South Africa and had proud feeling of being an African.

He justified the use of violence as,

> "I do not deny that I planned sabotage. I did not plan it in a spirit of recklessness or because I live violence…I planned it as a result of a calm and sober assessment of the political situation that had arisen after many years of tyranny, exploitation and oppression of my people by whites." (P-433)

He emphasized in the trial that ANC always stood for non-violence and non-racial democracy but nonviolence brought South Africans nothing but more repressive legislations and fewer rights. The people were talking of violence for long time but it was ANC who prevailed upon them to avoid violence and use peaceful methods. "Our policy (is) to achieve a nonracial state by non-violence." In a furious manner he questioned the court, "It has taken more than fifty years of the scars of the South African (Anglo Boer) war to disappear. How much longer would it take to eradicate the scars of inter-racial civil war?" (P-434) Nelson Mandela put his life on stake for the cause because he believed that this would boost struggle and would strengthen the cause. He initiated to defend his stand that if they received death sentence, they should not appeal it in higher court and accept the punishment. "An appeal would undermine the moral stance we had taken earlier." (P-444) His words were, "my death would be an inspiration to the cause for which I was giving my life." Nelson Mandela was ready to be a martyr like other revolutionary African historical and mythical leaders whose example he remembered and heard since his childhood and he quoted poetic lines of William Shakespeare as, "Be absolute for death, for either death or life shall be sweeter." (P-445) The court called out the case as 'the state against Nelson Mandela and others.' The court convicted him as guilty and in a judgment the court said,

> "All leaders of the non-European population were motivated entirely by a desire to ameliorate these grievances." The court stressed the word European and avoided the use of the word-whites. The judge added, "I am by no means convinced that the motives of the accused were as altruistic as they wish the court to believe. People who organize a revolution usually take over the government and personal ambition cannot be excluded as a motive." (P-447)

And the court penalize Nelson Mandela with life imprisonment on infamous Robben Island. The verdict was interpreted not as mercy of the whites but the international pressure as well as domestic. Dock workers around the world threatened to ban on South African goods. Russian Prime minister, fifty members of British Parliament, UNO, American Government all pressurized the Court not to give death penalty. Yet Nelson Mandela thought that they had accepted that they had not initiated guerrilla warfare. ANC and

MK were separate entities. The verdict brought new life in African struggle and it also untied the nation towards African nationalism. The jail started echoing the African singing freedom songs. The euphoria was seen everywhere around the nation and in jail each evening from dozen places throughout the prison men would yell "*Amandla*" and hundred voices replied, " *Ngawethu*." The voice of the nation became stronger.

Chapter Six

Robben Island: The dark years

Nelson Mandela personified the sacrifice of 'imprisonment' by staying longest term 27 years in jail as a political prisoner. After being proved guilty in Rivonia trial Nelson Mandela with six other prisoners were sentenced to infamous Robben Island jail. The jail was symbolized as "life in the shadow of death." On the arrival the jailor sarcastically welcomed them and added that they would come out of the jail in a year or two and return as national heroes, crowds would cheer for them and women and friend would want them everywhere. Mandela ironically stated, "Unfortunately his predictions proved to be out by nearly three decades." (P-454). He was taken to another Island after eighteen years. It was indeed a very long period in individual's life. He was taken away to different Island, he felt that Robben Island had become a part of his life. He was emotionally attached with that place. He felt too sensitive about the place that instead of celebrating his release he lamented whether he would ever see it again. He felt the indignities of the prison for not counting on the friendship bonds and loyalty with the prisoners as he was not allowed to meet his fellow prisoners with whom he shared his life for 18 years. Though he was sure that his home was Johannesburg but it was the place where he felt, "comfortable". Nelson Mandela went into jail as a radical revolutionary who felt violence as a preferred choice to attain his objective but he came out as more mature, meditative and humanist who could forgive his worst enemies and shake hands with the oppressors for the peaceful and harmonious life in South Africa. Robben Island proved a learning laboratory and place of spiritual transformation for him. "The challenge for every political prisoner is how to survive prison intact, how to emerge from prison undiminished, how to conserve and even replenish one's belief." (P-463) But prison was made to break one's spirit and destroy one's resolve. To destroy the spirit, the authorities attempted to exploit every weakness , destroy every initiative, neglect all signs of individuality- all with the idea of stamping out that spark that makes each of one as individual and the sense of being. But the hunter sometime shut in his own trap, the authorities tried to diminish their spirits, the inner strength of the prisoner it reverted into antithesis. It became more determinant and consolidated. Nelson Mandela understood that prison authorities conspired to rob each man's dignity and in the arena where he himself was the audience regarded the struggle as a microcosm of the struggle as whole.

As they were taken to the Island through a plane to Robben Island, the ANC prisoners watched the peninsula not as a tourist but as a strategist looking for areas for guerrilla warfare. They averred their happiness to find suitable terrine where they could fight with sophisticated whites. Nelson Mandela's contemplation always showed his deep love, care and vision of improvements for his own South Africa. Though he was kept far away from his land his mind and zeal never showed the distance as South Africa was very close to his heart.

In jail he became victim of racial harassments and apartheid injustice.

> " Robben Island was without question the hardest, most iron fisted outpost in South African penal system……the wardens were whites overwhelmingly Afrikaans speaking, demanded a master servant relationship….there were no black wardens and no white prisoner." P-459.

Africans were the most under privileged than colored and Indian prisoners. Like everything the diet was also discriminatory, the colored and Indians received a slightly better diet than Africans mixed with the remarks from the warden, "ag, you kaffirs are eating better in prison than you ever ate at home." P-466. His protested in the jail for full trousers like other prisoners. He eventually won. The idea of putting the ANC political prisoners on Island had more than one purpose. The obvious reason was to alienate them from the current boiling political happenings and making the organization orphan without leadership. The hidden purpose was to break the moral of the leaders by harsh and torturous physical as well as psychological exploitations to diminish their spirit. The hard work of breaking the stones, offering them stale and unhealthy food, humiliating treatment, isolating them from others and making them starve for minimal necessities were bestowed over them. Prisoners were permitted to write only a six hundred word letter every six months that too only to close family members. There was no clock to tell the time no calendar to point a day, month or year, "losing a sense of time is an easy way to lose one's grip and even one's sanity." Time seemed infinite and agonizing in prison as it never moved glacially, the demand for a toothbrush used to take six months or a year to be fulfilled. In prisoner Ahmad Khatrada's words, "in prison minutes can seem a year and years go by minutes." The classification of criminals to alphabetical group was inflexible feature of prison life. The highest classification conferred most privileges. Nelson Mandela being a special prisoner was deliberately put in D group and was considered as 'trouble maker' and marked to be always in the same group till his term. Even the miserable restriction were put by the authorities over prisoners. The anticipation of mail or letter was overwhelming but sometimes six month would go without mail. The mail was very dear and precious thing for a prisoner. The letters were not issued and when occasionally a letter would give the feeling of summer rain in the desert bloom. Nelson Mandela used to observe self-discipline not to explode with joy and would not give satisfaction to the authorities of seeing his eagerness. The letters were censored and would cut down the offending passages by razors and also cutting down the matter on the opposite side. He was refused to write a condolence letter to his lawyer who had lost his wife in a car accident. After three months on the island Nelson Mandela was told to have a visitor next day. They didn't disclose who was scheduled to visit. A politically banned person and his wife Winnie visited him on the island. She had to receive a special dispensation from the minister of justice. One day prior they used to inform suddenly that she had permission to see her husband tomorrow, this was enormously inconvenient.

Sometime authorities deliberately delayed issuing a permit until after the plane had departed. Poor family men did not see their wives for many years at a time if at all. He explained the hardships one followed as a prisoner at Robben Island.

He said,

> "I knew of men who spent a decade or more on Robben Island without a single visit. The visiting room had all sorts of inconvenience where a few small holes drilled into a wall to communicate, one had to talk very loudly to heard .It was tremendously frustrating not to be able to touch my wife, to speak tenderly to her , to have private moment together." P-477.

The conversation between him and Winnie happened in an awkward situation. Two wardens were constantly standing near them were keeping an eye closely on their movements. It was a feeling of uneasiness due to the presence of two warders standing directly behind her and him. Their role was to intimidate the conversation. African language was forbidden and conversation would be abruptly terminated if it involved any matter from politics. "time up" the warden yelled and the half an hour meeting ended leaving more agonies due to short time. Nelson Mandela bewailed his visit and his memory would return to that one visit again and again over next days, weeks, months. He knew he would not see her again for at least six months but the next visit came only after two years. The bad news from outside about families used to feel him helpless and forlorn. He missed wife and care for Winnie. Her absence made him feel 'powerless' and utter frustration surrounded him. The ban and arrest of Winnie had grief-stricken effects on him. In 1962 the political prisoners were assigned the toughest labor work on the lime quarry where he remained for next thirteen years. One had to break through the seashell and coral rock with extract the seam of lime with a shovel. That was most strenuous than the courtyard work. The transfer from courtyard to quarry was another way of enforcing discipline of showing that the political prisoners were not different than the other prisoners. Despite blistering and bleeding hands, Nelson Mandela felt invigorated around the beach in open air. Working there very hard in high temperature under burning sun was very hard punishment. By the evening all the prisoners looked like pale ghosts except where rivulets of sweat had washed away the lime. The request to allow them sunglasses was turned down by the authorities. His protest in the jail against the jail authorities continued. He protested for better facilities for the prisoners on humanitarian grounds. He always insisted on improving the prison conditions as a part of apartheid struggle, he spoke his attitude as,

> "It was in that sense all the same, we fought injustice wherever we found it, no matter how large or how small and we found it, no matter how large or how small and we fight injustice to preserve our own humanity."(P-482)

The other nuisances in the jail were the rowdy behavior of criminals and gangsters like *Big Five* or the *Twenty Eights* who used to terrorize other prisoners. They used to act '*agents provocateurs*' and they would fight, rag and push other prisoners for their entertainment. They used to push other prisoners around, take their food and inhabit their political debates. Even Walter Sisulu was victim of this. Nelson Mandela being mature and visionary politician involved with them and tried to communicate the cause of their struggle. He used it as an opportunity to bring different streams of ideologies and mold them for his mission. The gangsters and unlawful criminals, he found them, "raw material to be converted." (P-484) Nonpolitical prisoners from Robben Island like Joe who later joined ANC and was instrumental in smuggling material in and out of the prison. Nelson Mandela took initiative to patch up between oppositely poised parties like PAC. When PAC man Canya was beaten by the warder, Nelson Mandela proposed a case in head office for him and made the authorities to remove the culprit from the island. In other case Bogart the PAC man who was beaten by the warden and he fetched Nelson Mandela's legal help. But he turned hostile in the court and took back all the charges.

Nelson Mandela due to his political image and leadership qualities naturally emerged as a leader amongst all prisoners and he performed his lawful duty towards his fellow prisoners. He was pure humanist who helped everybody to reconcile. When two International press journalists visited Robben Island, he became the spoke person of the prisoners. He raised objection on their visiting each one individually. "When the authorities needed the prisoner to speak on the behalf of others that individual would be me." (P-470) He fearlessly encountered the panel of Mr. Newman and raised several issues against the authorities regarding 'inhuman treatments and conditions' on the Island. These allegations embarrassed the government. In another visit of Mr. Hynning a

British lawyer and representative of American Bar Associations, jail authorities wanted to keep Nelson Mandela away from him and asked the prisoners to select their representative but the prisoners unanimously called out Nelson Mandela's name. It was obvious that there was a great concern about the conditions of the prisoners outside world and the authorities were keen to show that everything was all right.

High Organ- Prisoner's Organization

To address the grievances of the prisoners and mobilize the prisoners over the Island, Nelson Mandela initiated an organization on the line of ANC named as *High Organ*. It was decided unanimously that *High Organ* would make decisions on the prisoner's behalf but would not try to influence external ANC policy. The *High Organ* would make decisions about such matters as prisoner's complaints, strikes, mail, food, and all the day to concerns of prison life. The work would be carried out secretly as it was very dangerous from official point of view. The meetings would be held secretly and the decisions would be communicated to all prisoners. High Organ also acted as a representative committee for all the political prisoners in their section. In 1967 the committee organized a petition demanding better treatment that was signed virtually by everyone including the members of PAC, Unity Movement and the liberal Party represented by Eddie Daniels. The committee later on later on named as "Ulundi" and acted as disciplinary committee for all the prisoners and the leadership would be kept on rotational basis. High Organ confronted some controversies because of its ethnic composition as all four permanent members were from Xhosa background. Nelson Mandela was displeased with the Xhosa domination as he himself belonged to the same tribe. To refute the issue he reassured that ANC had given all tribes equal opportunity to lead, there were leaders from Zulu, Basotho, Pedis and Tswanas communities. His efforts made to formulate the natural principle that discrimination or domination in any form must be crippled and he decided that there should be fifth rotating member of the High Organ who would not be Xhosa. Two issues came up for the debate amongst the prisoner leaders. The first was the prison regulations stated that prisoners must stand in the presence of senior officer which Nelson Mandela protested and felt that they should be seated and express the self-esteem of political prisoners but other members of the organization felt that it was a trivial issue. The second issue was regarding calling the name of the prisoner's. Nelson Mandela felt that the warder must add honorific 'Mr.' for the political prisoners but other prisoners did not gave it an importance. Nelson Mandela reversed his stance and accepted that the issue was not very urgent and important. It showed his flexibility in retreating back. It was the quality of a visionary leadership.

Prison and Outside news.

Authorities of the jail were purposely attempting to cut of the prisoners from outside world and alienated them from all the happenings from their families, societies and nation. The prisoner were very keen and curious about the news within and outside the jail. Newspaper for a prisoner was more valuable than anything else,

> "Newspapers are more valuable to political prisoners than gold and diamonds. More hungered for it than food or tobacco. They were the most precious contraband on the prison. News was the intellectual raw material of the struggle. As the prisoners were craving the News and authorities were strictly banning it….Walter even more than myself seemed to bereft without news.(P-492)

The authorities attempted complete imposition and complete blackout about news coming from outside world. They did not want the prisoners to learn anything that might arise their moral or reassure them that people on the outside world were still thinking about them. Over the years, they devised many ways of obtaining the news but their efforts didn't bear fruits. Warder's rapped material newspaper page would be retrieved out of the dust bin and the matter was shared amongst all. There was tremendous hunger for news and they used to fulfill the hunger for the news by any means. Nelson Mandela admitted that he paid bribe to the warder for newsletters. "The only area where I tolerated what were often unethical means of obtaining information." (P-492) The warder's poverty was prisoner's opportunity. Possessions of newspaper by any prisoner was a serious charge. The paper was destroyed once it was read secretly and the brief summary of the news was circulated amongst the prisoners. One day Nelson Mandela noticed a newspaper and as he started reading by forgetting the watchdogs, he was caught by the warder. He didn't offer a defense and was sentenced to three days in isolation and deprivation of meals.

Nelson Mandela didn't disclose the name of the warder who supplied the newspaper. He protected the warder and expressed his loyalty and gratitude towards the warder.

The punishments were innovated to break the moral of the prisoner. One of such punishment was isolation and deprivation of meal. The punishment was the deprivation of company, exercise and recreations and it would result self-dooming. As a punishment in trivial issue Nelson Mandela served three days term and went without food for three days through the agonies of it. The first day went over with the severest pain and agonies as the body was accustomed to eating regularly and was not used to such challenge. He did not like the idea of hunger strike that Mahatma Gandhi practiced as Satyagraha. But showed his dislikes with the method and outcome of hunger strike. The hunger strike was demonstrated in the prison at different occasion against the authorities and it went on successfully yet Nelson Mandela was not happy about it as he said, " the advocates of hunger strike argued that it was a traditionally accepted form of protest that has been waged all over the world by such prominent leader as Mahatma Gandhi." (p-503) For him hunger strike was 'altogether too passive' and the rationale behind them was always "struck me quixotic." The basic condition of hunger strike was that the outside world must learn of it. For him hunger strike was as down as begging the favor from the cruel oppressor and losing the self-esteem which violence proclaims.

In July 1966 Nelson Mandela participated in a hunger strike to support the general prisoners who had organized it to protest against the poor conditions prevailing in the jail. Nelson Mandela's support was not based on principle but on the indivisibility and unity of all prisoners. The authorities were dividing the prisoners by disinformation and campaigned the sections against each other. The hunger strike organized by general prisoners created a mass participation and the whole prison was united against the authorities. The five day hunger strike was successfully ended as on the last fifth day the warders also participated. The prisoners and authorities were knelt on their knees. The combination of the two strikes was too more for the authorities and they suggested the prisoners to form a committee of three prisoners to delegate the talks with them. It was indeed a moral victory and caused the unanimity amongst all. But Nelson Mandela was apprehensive about the hunger strike movement because the success of it depends upon the masses how they would get sparked for action. "Hunger strike would elicit newspaper stories which in turn would generate pressure from support groups."(P-503) He admitted that he favored a more militant style of protest such as work strike, go slow strike, refusing to clean up, actions that punished the authorities not themselves. The purpose of the strike should be to punish the adamant authorities and not getting troubled with our own behavior. "This kind of behavior distressed and exasperated them whereas I think they secretly enjoyed watching us go hungry." (P-503) Even he realized that all prisoners could not participate in the strike as it might not be bearable for some. One of a prisoner colleague expressed his inability to participate. But some comrades would sometime eat on sly.

Sad news and moments of breaking down

One of the most painful and heart breaking moments during the imprisonment on Robben Island were not those of hardest and toughest work of breaking stones or humiliating moments but the sad family news and the feeling of his powerlessness as a head of the family. The bad news about the deaths of his friend and associate Bram Fisher's wife Molly Fisher shook him with distress. Fisher was his lawyer and fellow struggler whose wife in his word, "wonderful, generous, unselfish and utterly without prejudice" (P-462) It was shattering a moment. He couldn't see her for last time. In addition to his pains, he was denied to write few line of condolence to Bram Fisher. The news about the harassments and tortures of his beloved wife frequently devastated him. Prison robbed his family life and all those happy moments one spends with family. He often lamented in the dark chamber of his room alone. When Winnie came to meet him for the first time on Robben Island, he was deprived of "seeing her beautiful face and her new and elegant look." (P-477) Later he came to know about her dismissal from her job at child welfare office. He felt it very sorrowful because he knew that she was loving her job as a social worker. He described his pains as, "The banning and harassment of wife greatly troubled me. I could not looked after my children and the state was making it difficult for her to look after herself. My powerlessness groaned me." (P-477).

In 1968 the telegram informed Nelson Mandela about the death of his mother. It was the saddest moment as he recollected it with utmost pain. The government refused him permission to bury his own mother as the only and eldest son. Nelson Mandela faced many blows from destiny but as a professional boxer he defended and recorded victory over them but the blow of his mother's death was the most tragic punch he got in his life time. Mother's death left him forlorn with pain and the feeling of disowning the family responsibilities made him to feel guilty. As the eldest son of the family he thought that he should have paid more attention to her and should have given support and comfort in her last days.

He recollected all her pains for bringing him up from the poverty and provided support to him for education and practice of law. As a freedom fighter he performed his duty and kept national interest before family interest "putting the people's welfare even before that of my own family." He realized that those were the decisions a freedom fighter ought to make in his life for the cause of the people. "In South Africa, it is hard for a man to ignore the needs of the people even at the expenses of his own family." (P-529). He suffered agonies as a son and said that, " I felt regret that I had not been able to look after her properly during her life and a longing for what might have been able had I chosen to live my life differently." (P-695)

He showed his gratitude towards his comrade Bram Fisher, who was no more and the news pained a lot. Nelson Mandela owed a lot and always mentioned him. His death affected him deeply, "No matter what I suffered in my pursuit of freedom, I always took strength from the fact that I was fighting with and for my own people." (P-562)

Another very mournful news that hit him in the jail after his mother's death was the telegram he received as, "The eldest son, the first son Madiba Thembekile had been killed in a car accident in Trankskie……it left a whole in my heart that can never be filled."(P-531) Nelson Mandela asked for permission to attend his son's funeral which was denied even a letter of condolence to his first wife was not permitted. These sacrifices made him a man of highest fortitude. These fatal blows of sad family member's death agonized him but they also made him strong to face life and made him internally strong.

Chapter Seven

Robben Island--Beginning of Hope

The incident that happened 1969 were titled as "Beginning of new hope" He started feeling new hope. The darkest hour of his personal tragedies seemed to be over and the hope brought him nearer to his goal. As natural law the darkest hour is always followed with a glowing dawn, the darkest hour was in the destiny of South Africa and Nelson Mandela and the dawn was at the waiting. The first positive change was the conditional change in prisoner's life " (conditions) did improve." After Van Resburg's departure the life on Island became "more tolerable". Prisoners received personal uniform. They were given boards and cards to play on Saturdays and Sundays. Warders became friendlier and the authorities were little softer.

Religion in prison

Speaking his views on religion he admitted that, " though I am a Methodist, I would attend each different religious service." And added that "stern and god fearing Africans takes his religion seriously."(P-536) Ironically the immoralist and oppressors who were Christian by religion considered Sunday prayers mandatory for prisoners. Father Hughes, an Anglican priest who preached them as well as entertained them with radio address from Winston Churchill. But Reverend Jones who tried to preach what he didn't practice. He preached importance of reconciliation. He was intermediated as, "implying that it was we who needed to reconcile ourselves to the whites." And Eddie Daniels told Jones that "We have been seeking reconciliation for the last seventy five years." (P-537) Reverend Scheffer was an unorthodox preacher who adopted scientific approach to religion which Nelson Mandela found "appealing". Science was often used to eradicate the supernatural claims of religion but he used science to bolster his belief. He gave many parallels between bible and science. He also pointed out black dichotomy towards whites humorously,

> "The white man has a more difficult task than the black man in the country whether there is a problem, we have to find a solution. But whenever black have a problem you have an excuse. You can simply say "Ingabilunga" which in Xhosa means, "It is the whites." (P-538)

Humanitarian attitude with jailor

The new jailor Badenhorst's arrival on the Island was an alarm of terror. He was reputed to be one of the most brutal authoritarian officer in the entire prison service. The authorities always wanted the prisoners to suffer. Nelson Mandela boldly confronted him on several occasions showing to him that his intimidating and formidable spirit was not worn off. In the case of brutal beating of a general prisoner, Nelson Mandela appeared in front of the three judge panel and represented himself as a prime witness to give justice to the ordinary. His arduous nature was nurtured with various challenges he accustomed in prison. He withstood Badenhorst's warning in front of the judges and enumerated many complaints about diet, work and studying. This bold move initiated transfer of Badenhorst whose regime was the perhaps the most barbaric and callous they had had on Robben Island. But at the farewell he spoke nice words to Nelson Mandela and wished him good luck. Nelson Mandela evaluated the human behavior in the humanitarian context and realized the philosophic truth, "It was a useful reminder that all men even the most seemingly cold blooded have a core of decency and that if their heart are touched, they are capable of changing." P-549. Mandela always believed in the good human side of the person which he exhibited himself and treated more humanly. When new head of the prison Colonel Willemse joined he consulted Mandela and sought his help in controlling his men to restore order and discipline. That was a paradigm shift in authorities approach towards him. But forgetting previous enmity and revenge he proactively organized the meeting of all prisoners and addressed them, "At least appear to be working at a pace suitable to us." P-551. This win-win strategy was a successful tactics which ultimately resulted into his reconciliation of whites and blacks. Nelson Mandela was heart winner. He handled the tensely situations in very tactical manner. He responded the situation whenever it needed. He applied his tactical harmonious tactics. He won the hearts of colleagues and his closest enemies.

As a lawyer he observed that in South Africa law didn't guarantee a defendant the right to representation and thousands and thousands of indignant men and women went to prison every year for lack of such representation. Hardly few Africans afforded a lawyer. In jail he would receive a smuggled note asking for help. A consultation that would take a year or more on the island. He advised his clients to write a letter to the registrar of the Supreme Court asking for the record of the case with an appeal. He used to help the clients in all possible ways to bring justice, "Prison is contrived to make one feel powerless and this was one of the ways to move the system" p-558.

In the year 1972 Nelson Mandela came to know about the ransacking and arresting of Winnie by police and she was charged her with six years imprisonment. Winnie wrote a letter to him reaffirming her commitment in the freedom struggle. The struggle was kept continuing inside the jail by Nelson Mandela and outside by Winnie. His grown up daughters wished to see him but they were denied permission on the ground of their immature age. He lamented the situation, "It is a source of deep sorrow not to be able to see one's children." P-559. With the fake and fabricated birth certificates, the daughters were able to see Nelson Mandela in jail. Meeting to his daughter was one of the happiest moment in his life. The meeting after a decade and half with his own daughters unfolded his sacrifice and immensely loving father. Though he was stubborn revolutionary but daughter's love made him to be very sensitive. He made her feel comfortable and tried to look young and happy. He uttered, "I could see her holding back her tears as I talked" P-561. A loving father tied into the shackles of his commitment.

Plans of escape from jail

Being in prison Nelson Mandela inspired millions of countrymen and the struggle was kept alive with this. He was not active outside but certainly his absence also accounted in the struggle. The people of South Africa would be with him all the time he was assured. Yet he found himself powerless in the prison and was totally out of his organization. His goal to uproot apartheid seemed too long to achieve. Escaping from Robben Island was impossible. The fear getting caught while absconding would be a suicide. But they never left that option closed. His colleagues Mac Maharaj and Eddie Daniels hatched several plans though they were risky. They attempted to make a duplicate key but didn't get an opportunity to use it. "It was the sea after all that was the non-crossable mountain around Robben Island." P-565.

In 1974 they actually planned to abscond with Mac Maharaj's plan from dentist office at Cape Town what they thought as "the best chance of actually executing an escape." P-565 But at the last moment they acknowledged, "It's a trap." Another truly unimaginable and impractical idea was suggested by Eddie, "To use helicopter and deposit Mandela on the friendly foreign embassy in Cape Town." Nelson Mandela couldn't escape unofficially but he was offered officially to get released 'conditionally'. Jimmy Kruger, the minister of prison and influential and important minister of the government said, "Mandela you ought to retire to the Transkei and take long rest." It sounded that his freedom must be compensated with retirement from freedom struggle. It could have given him personal victory but it would be betrayal of all South Africans which he never accepted. Kruger's proposal was direct and clear,

"He stated the matter simply: if I recognize the legitimacy of Transkei Government and was willing to move there, my sentence would be dramatically reduced." (P-574) He kept his temper firm and asserted his commitment and devotion to South Africa as he reiterated, "I was from Johannesburg and it was to Johannesburg that I would return." (P-574)

Agitations all over the nation

Jail authorities tried to keep the prisoners away from latest happening in the country still news used to come and reach the prisoners from many sourses. The big news they come to know about the nationwide agitations and Governments unsuccessful efforts to curb them. They were rejoiced to know that on 16th July 1976 fifteen thousands of school children agitated against Government demanding Africans languages to be included in their curriculum. The agitations were marked by the police brutality against the adolescent students who were beaten down and open firing on the students eventually killing a student named Hector Pieterson and many other students. Two white personnel were also killed in retaliation. The country was reverberated in every town of South Africa. The isolation section in the prison started swelling with young prisoners who were getting arrested voluntarily. Nelson Mandela and his fellow comrades were delighted to see the spirit of the people and mass protest. He happily said that "There is nothing so encouraging in prison as learning that the people outside are supporting the cause for which you are inside."(P-576)

The new and immature breed of prisoners had an instinct to confront rather than co- operate. This was not expected by Nelson Mandela. They even disregarded the senior leaders by ignoring their call for discipline and overlooked their advice as feeble and unassertive. The commanding officer sought Nelson Mandela's help to discipline them but he refused to mediate as these young men would have regarded him as "collaborator of oppressor". The young prisoners belonged to Black Consciousness Movement which came into existence after ANC, PAC and Communist parties were banned by the government. It was a product of political vacuum created by these banning. The BCM was less movement oriented and more philosophical. Those young men wanted to liberate themselves from psychological inferiority complex amongst blacks. Nelson Mandela appreciated their militancy approach but disregarded their claim of forming a non-racial society without whites. He felt that their attitude was immature and the root of it was found in operating style of the Government. The oppressiveness of the government resulted into Black Consciousness Movement. He reported his dissatisfaction on the functioning of BMC for "no program of action and no outlet for their protest."

The Image of Leader

He performed the role friend,guide and philosopher to all heterogeneous ideological parties like PAC, BMC, Communist party in counseling them towards humanity and unity. His image had emerged as great leader who had done supreme sacrifice. He had earned authority with his commendable behavior. He created strong trust and respect amongst the all parties of different background in South Africa. He always played a role of unifier and tried to bring all under harmony and good will. He narrated this in his own words, "I regarded my role in prison as not just the leader of ANC but a promoter of unity, an honest broker of peacemaker." (P-580) He always relished his earthly rooting as a Xhosa tribe and always grounded his feet into soil of his land. He was an earthly man who knew his people, land and culture very well and had pride for it. He found that the Whites had lost their earthly connections and hence lost their humanity. They were not only outsiders but also unearthly and that's why they were brutal in their approach. He never felt the western hegemony with sense of inferiority complex. Nelson Mandela's style of playing chess reveals his political moves,

> "I considered the mummifications of every option and took a long time between moves. I resist such analogies not only in draughts but in politics." P-539. What he preached echoed in his meditations on leadership "for a leader must temper justice with mercy." (P-541)

Hobbies and interests of a person reflects his idiosyncrasies and internal mold of his thought process and philosophical dimensions. Nelson Mandela had kept boxing as his hobby in his initial years. It showed his formidability and toughness of his attitude. He was a born fighter with the powerful body and mind. His physical endurance and mantle strength to undergo all sort of challenges could be owed to the hobby of boxing. But under that rocky and stubborn fighter a soft, emotional and purely human soul was hidden.

In jail asked for a permission to his long presumed hobby of gardening. In the dry and rocky court yard soil he planted small saplings of beautiful flowers. It is a symbolic behavior. Under the brutal oppressive jail system he had not lost hope for future. He cultivated the beauty on barren land which had lost all the hopes. He metaphorically added that gardening was,

> "I saw garden as a metaphor for certain aspects of life. A leader must also tend his garden, he too sows seeds and then watches, cultivates and harvests the result. I like the gardener, a leader must take responsibility for what he cultivates. He must mind his work, try to repel enemies, preserve what can be preserved and eliminate that cannot succeed." (P-583)

His gratitude didn't end only to his nation, people who were associated with him or only blacks but it crossed all the barriers of color, oppressor –oppressed and admitted that white South African writers particularly, " all the unbanned novels of Nadine Gordimer and learned a greater deal about the white liberal sensitivity." P-585.

Meeting the daughter Zinzdi after 21 years

Winnie Mandela faced tough times in the absence of her husband. The banning, harassments, arrests had tortured her throughout her life. The news about her gave very helpless feelings to Nelson

Mandela. His daughter Zinzdi now turned to twenties was also under the watch of the Government. Being the daughter of Nelson Mandela couldn't get any better treatment by the authorities. Zinzdi's harassments vindicated the fact that authorities were still biased and prejudiced about blacks and even after a generation Governments attitude had not changed by a percent. Zinzdi like her father became a political activist was kept under police surveillance by the Government. The interim harassment resulted in her banning. Affidavits filed before the court described policeman bursting into the house and threatening Zinzdi. He was keen on the news about her. As a father he suffered to hear her harassments by the Government. He thought that every freedom fighter had to pay some cost for protesting against the government.

Getting disconnected from family and family responsibilities was most lamenting thoughts that came in his mind. He couldn't recollect how many the small incidents of love and apathy were missed. But though he was away from family the love between daughter and him didn't vanish. She must have kept her father's memories alive in his absence. When Zini his second daughter turned 21 years and came to see him she literally ran and embraced her father. The moment was full of emotionally loaded and he added, "It was dizzying experience as though time had sped forward as a science fiction novel." He groaned for his lost time that he spent without the love of his family. The moment he held his grand baby daughter in his hand he mourned "Hands that for too long had held only picks and shovel." P- 589.

Hope of new dawn

He named his daughter as "Zaziwe" which means a "hope." He was firmly believed with that his sacrifice and struggle would not go in vain. Out of the extinguished hopes of the past would arise new wave of freedom and his next generation would be creating the new nonracial South Africa on that darkest past. His generation had suffered the pains of apartheid but he dreamed hope for next generation. "I was convinced that this child would be a part of new generation of South Africa for whom apartheid would be a distant memory- that was my dream." Nelson Mandela's words resembles the words of Martin Luther King Jr. when he proclaimed his famous speech "I have a dream." In the entire journey of life Nelson Mandela never lost hope. He gave hopes to others. Hope of new dawn. Hope of bright future. Hope of non-racial South Africa. Hope of better tomorrow was visible due to the sacrifice of many. His hope that came from the darkest hours of his life. His dream seemed very close when he saw a positive change in the thawing relationship between blacks and whites in the hospital where he was treated in humanistic atmosphere. He reiterated that only good education would eradicate the long held belief of prejudice. Instead of relying on religion and inner change Nelson Mandela relied on science that would bring change in the attitude of the people. In the jail hospital he was treated by white doctors and nurses. He felt that "These were the men of science and science had no room for racism." (P-603)

Chapter- Eight

Talking with the Enemy

When Nelson Mandela was taken to Robben Island in 1964 he thought that, "I was forty six years old a political prisoner with a life sentence and small cramped space was to be my home for I knew not how long" (P-456). The answer to his question of his release came up in 1982 after eighteen years of his imprisonment. He was shifted in Pollsmoor prison near Cape-town. The political tactic of shifting him from Robben Island to Pollsmoor was unknown to him and his ANC comrades. All believed that the authorities were attempting to cut off the head of the ANC on the island by removing its leadership. "Robben Island itself was becoming a sustaining myth in the struggle." (P-612) The authorities wanted to rob some of its symbolic important by removing it. Different important leaders were also joined him Walter, Raymond, Mlangeni, Kathy, Patrick and Maqubela. The political turmoil was on its high all over South Africa.

Bombing by MK

In December 1982 MK organization set off explosions at the unfinished Iceberg nuclear power plant outside Cape Town and placed bombs at mainland and other places. Nelson Mandela's transfer from one jail to another was protested with internal and external forces. MK's bomb blasts and the banning and sanctions from other countries isolated and pressured the government. MK's bombing helped the struggle and put tremendously extra pressure on Government though the method they used was violent and condemnable. MK's first car bomb killed nineteen people and injured two hundred. In governments retaliation Nelson Mandela's comrade Ruth was killed whose wife was also freedom fighter. Nelson Mandela felt horror about the things and happenings but he advocated that violence was necessary sometime to retaliate violence. "Human fallibility is always a part of war and the price of it always high… the armed struggle was imposed upon us by the violence of the apartheid regime." (P-618)

The Government and ANC started working parallels on two roads. One way was the military way which would lead towards violence and other was political that would lead towards nonviolence. The Government pursued 'divide and rule' policy by offering Indians and colored some representation in the parliament dueling and diving from Africans.

United Democratic front another subsidiary party branch by ANC became very popular and blossomed into a powerful organization. It had over six hundred anti-apartheid organizations including trade unions, community groups, church groups and student associations. The organization experienced a new birth of popularity, emerging as the most popular political organization despite of facing a ban nearly for quarter of a century. Anti-apartheid caught attention of the world. The popularity and solidarity of the organization resulted into 1984's Nobel peace award to Desmond Tutu, the ANC loyalist and close friend of Nelson Mandela.

Lord Bethel discussed the situation with Nelson Mandela about the armed struggle in the country and asked him to "renounce violence". Nelson Mandela discussed the offer positively and he clarified his role that it was not up to ANC but up to the government to stop the violence.

Terrorist or Moderate

In his interview to Washington Times which had biased western out-look about Nelson Mandela. The media labeled him as "communist and a terrorist". He reiterated that "I was neither a communist nor a terrorist". They attempted to show that I was not Christian either by asserting that Reverend Martin Luther king never resorted to violence." (P-620)

Nelson Mandela was labelled as military activist and it was very hard to convince the moderates and liberates that he was not a communist or terrorist. He told the press reporter that the conditions in USA for Martin Luther King Jr was different than his own conditions. United States was a democracy with constitutional guarantees of equal rights. The constitution was there to protect non-violent protests and agitations against government. There was prejudice and atrocities against blacks. South Africa on the other hand was a police state with a constitution that enshrined inequality and army to demolish non-violence with force. The conditions could not be compared in any form.

Nelson Mandela never advocated his Christian belongings. His opponents, the White regime also belonged to the same religion. In

Martin Luther King's case, he was a reverend and had strong Christian background. Reverend King symbolized religion as a tool to mobilize and unite people. The conditions were favorable with democracy liberal press and constitutional rights favored King Jr to use Christianity with successes.

"I was a Christian and always had been a Christian. But even Christ used force to expel the moneylenders from the temple----he had no choice but to use force against evil."(P-620).

Offer of release

The Government authorities were under tremendous pressure regarding the release of Nelson Mandela but they were not ready to proceed talk. They wanted to work out the things on their terms though the pressures from home and abroad were intensifying.

The government tactically made public announcement on 31st Jan 1985 to offer Nelson Mandela freedom if he unconditionally rejects violence as a political instrument. Government jeopardized the situation as a challenge by stating that it was not the government stand in the way of Mr. Nelson Mandela freedom but he himself.

It was the "sixth conditional offer" that the government made in last ten years. The offer was also viewed as an attempt to drive a wedge between Nelson Mandela and his colleagues. The secret negotiations with Nelson Mandela were deliberately arranged to spread the rumor that he was taking over the ANC. He always wanted to reassure the ANC in general and Oliver Tambo in particular that his loyalty to the organization was beyond a question. His final comment on all happenings was that. "Negotiations not was the path to a solution." (P-621).

His written speech given to his daughter Zinzdi to read a front of the cheering crowd of UDF in a stadium. The speech reiterated " I am not a violent man-It was when all other forms of resistance were no longer open to us that we turned to armed struggle." (P-622). He clearly supported his own people and ANC that he too supported nonviolence but the government had not left them any way but to choose violence. The situation was heading towards no solution. South Africans had fought against white minority rule for three quarters of a century and armed struggle was operative for two decades that was relatively new. The enemy was strong and resolute with all machinery against blacks who had only advantage of being in majority. He knew the fact that military action would not be a solution of the problem.

> "It was a clear to me to me that a military victory was a distant if not possible dream. It simply did not make any sense on both sides to lose thousands if not millions of lives in a conflict that was unnecessary-----It was a time to talk."(P-626).

Talks for resolution

The first formal meeting of the secret working groups took place in May 1988. The talks were resumed on the behalf of ANC but the ANC members was dispersed in various countries or had gone underground. There was no core leader available to represent

ANC. To resume the talks was impossible. It was the most crucial decision for Nelson Mandela whether to wait for all ANC members to come and contribute or to go alone and take up the responsibility. It was all left to him to take a call on these issues. He was firm and confident about the turns of the events. "There are times when a leader must move out ahead of the lock, go off in new direction confident that he is leading his people the right way".(P-627). Finally official talks was resumed.

The preliminary rounds of debates went in tasting the water from both sides. Nelson Mandela came to know that Government had no knowledge about ANC and they had prejudices and negative opinions about ANC. The four issues were on consensus. The four primary issues put on the table with priorities were the concerns for resolving the armed struggle, the ANC's alliance with community party, the goal of majority rule and the idea of racial reconciliation.

Authorities wanted ANC to prohibit the violence because it was nothing more than criminal behavior and could not be tolerated by state. The fact convinced Nelson Mandela that the state was afraid of violence and the talks were on the table only for this reason. Violence became tactical issue which Nelson Mandela acknowledged and he did not gave any promice on violence to bend the rigid government to their terms. Nelson Mandela could not promise them to stop of violence. He stated, "The state was responsible for the violence and that it is the oppressor not the oppressed who dictates the form of struggle" (P-641).

Clarifying his stand on second important issue of ANC and Nelson Mandela's stand on communism, he convinced them at greater length that ANC was a national party and owe to South Africa. The communist party was outsiders and they were rivals in their long term interests of the nation. But the short term common goal for both the parties was to overthrow the racial oppression and the birth of non-racial South Africa.

The white authorities were concerned about their capitalist estates and particularly afraid of communism ideology. Nelson Mandela found the mean and insisted that the South African were for a more even distribution of the rewards of the certain industries. Nationalization might occur in some of those areas but he referred to an article he wrote in 1956 for Liberation. He had said that the freedom charter was not the blue print of socialism but for "African Capitalism" and reinterred his past position. He showed his flexibility in the negotiations. The authority were more skeptical about the white representation in new nonracial South Africa and were concerned about their rights as the white minority. Nelson Mandela referred them with the preamble of freedom charter: "South Africa belongs to all who live in it, blacks and whites" (P-643).

Twist and turns in negotiations

Nelson Mandela epitomized truth and faith of not only blacks but also of whites. He knew that unless whites feel confidence, the new nonracial South Africa could not come into reality. The feeling of revenge against white had to be removed and blacks needed to see them with love. Other parties had different opinion. They wanted all powers in the hands of black and the decisions would be made after that. He did not agree with the later.

The breakthrough in negotiations was not easy. It was a mind game of centuries and heavily loaded with historical burdens and the piles of prejudices. The authorities were dealing with Nelson Mandela because they felt he was the voice of South African prolonged struggle. He was the one who could be believed and trusted. He was a man who represented ANC and could convince ANC to accept the terms. His stature was greater than any other leader at present.

Though Nelson Mandela alone was dealing on the behalf of his comrades at Dolls moor and Robben Island and Lusaka. He had a feeling that "Although I know I was going ahead of my colleagues, I did not want to go too far and find that I was all alone" (P-653).

The deadlock continued for a longer period of time though the negotiations were going on with meetings after meetings. Two political issues were the point of concern. First the demand for majority rule in a democratic state. Secondly the concern of white South Africans who were skeptical over this demand.

The negotiations were interrupted by the delay. In January P. W. Botha the President suffered a stroke. Political violence and international pressure intensified. Political detainers had held a successful hunger strike forcing the authorities to release over nine-hundred prisoners from jails. Mass Democratic Movement (MDM) was organized by the people of South Africa "defiance campaign of civil dis-obedience to challenge apartheid institutions". Gandhian way was adopted by the South Africans.

Family matters

Nelson Mandela came to know his wife's violent methods of vengeance and revenge against the authorities. Winnie with an immature violent group of young so called bodyguard became involved in violent activities that were unbecoming be a liberation struggle. That deeply perplexed Nelson Mandela because he knew with his political experience that such a scandalous behavior only serve to divide the movement at time when unity was essential. It was politically crucial moment to take a stance. He asserted his support to his wife by saying, "I wholly supported my wife maintained that while she had shown poor judgement she was innocent of any serious charges." (P-655).

His birthday had become a symbolic political day of festivity since he became public figures in South Africa. For the people of South Africa it was an important day to pay their tribute and to exhibit gratitude to their leaders. His seventy fifth birthday was celebrated with the entire family. It was the first time that he ever had his wife, children and grandchildren all in one place. It was a moment of highest pleasure to have his whole family around him but the only pain was he had missed such occasions for so many years.

A call of meeting

The most historic moment of the anti-apartheid struggle came on 4 July when the white supreme President Botha sent a courtesy call to Nelson Mandela. Finally the Government acknowledged Nelson Mandela as the correct and true leader of people. He was the biggest trouble maker and enemy to them. Before the meeting he was treated most graciously than ever by the commanding officers who were taking him to the meeting. Major Marais helping him meticulously to wear the tie neatly and Dr. Barnard literally knot down to tie his shoe less. These courtesies symbolically attributed the changed scenario and the power of time President P. W. Botha reputedly known as crocodile for his hot temperament but he showed completely disarmed attitude towards Nelson Mandela. The new President who replaced Botha, de Klerk continued the same policy and permitted a peaceful march of the people to take place in the country. It was the first friendly treatment and hospitality towards the people of South Africa shown by the Government. Nelson Mandela reported "A new and different hand was on the tiller."(P-660).

February 2 1990 pinned the victorious moment when F. W. de Klerk in his parliamentary speech did something no other South African head had ever done-the bans of ANC, PAC, communist party were lifted, "It was a defining moment in the anti- apartheid movement."

The life sentence imprisonment for Nelson Mandela was declared cancelled and he would be released from the prison after serving 27 years jail. The day and place was not decided but Nelson Mandela proposed the place 'Victor Vorster' and the Government agreed to his demand.

Chapter- Nine

Freedom

> "It was this desire for the freedom of my people to live their lives with dignity and self-respect that animated my life that transformed a frightened young man into a bold one, that drove a law abiding attorney to become a criminal that turned a family loving husband into a man without a home that forced a life loving man to live like a monk."(P-750).

Finally Nelson Mandela was released from the It was not just a moment of coming out of seclusion but it was a metaphoric historical moment for him as well as entire nation and world. He wanted his "Ten thousand days" brutal punishment to count each move he inclined with a desirable effect. He inclined to spend his first night in Cape Town "to show my solidarity – the busting black and colored township" but eventually for other reasons he spent his night at Desmond Tutu's home in posh white area – symbolizing an open compassion towards non-racialism. His release created a euphoria and the day was marked with the beginning of a new hope to all is South Africa. At the moment of his coming out of jail and media asked him to "walk towards freedom." It was filmed - at the age of seventy one he realized "that my life was beginning a new my ten thousand days of imprisonment were at last over"(p-673).When the people were crowding on the roads and terraces to get the glimpse of their "greatest hero" Nelson Mandela on his way stopped at a point and got out of the car to greet and thank one such white family and tell them, "how inspired I was by their support" (P-674).

He observed the South Africa had gone through tremendous changes since his going into jail. Nelson Mandela was among the best orator of the world who used his resources of orator skills to steer the public emotions violently. In his speech he touched upon the emotions of the people saying, "South Africans I great you all in the name of peace, democracy and freedom for all".(p-676).

Time and again his speeches, press conferences and interviews were marked with faith and trust. He asserted his unequivocal support for the "Comrade struggle." He advocated violence because he believed that this tactic brought the government on the table of negations but he ultimately knew that "peace" is the only option all had left with "Freedom without civility freedom without the ability to live in peace was not true freedom at all"(p-681). He dispensed the critical role for whites. He reiterated ANC's stand that whites are fellow Africans whites would not be left out in any political system.

The difficult times

But soon he understood that the long walk to freedom had not come to its destination but it would become more complex, more breath taking and dangerous at times His release on 11/02/90 and his taking over as President on 10th may 1994 those four years were the most crucial days in South Africa's history.

When new order enters into its beginning or an era starts into the history of new nation, the phase was always very euphoric. The country economically politically and morally oppressed was not meant to face the democratic fulfillment so easily and naturally. On the political map of South Africa, Chief Buthelezi head of Inkatha Freedom Party and the Chief Minister of Kwazuler were one of the primer players and natural rivals to Nelson Mandela in popularity and authority. He didn't want to bargain on his nuisance value. He opposed armed struggle, criticized 1976 Soweto uprising, campaigned against International sanctions and opposed the idea of unity of South Africa. The king was the true hereditary leader of the Zulus.

In Natal, heavily armed Inkatha supporters openly targeted ANC people. In March 1990 more than 200 people were killed in violence. During negotiations with Mr. de klerk, violence in Johannesburg erupted and police fired twelve men to death. Nelson Mandela announced his suspension of "talks with the government" and sternly warned Mr. de klerk that "talk about negotiations on the one hand and murder our people on the other" could not be tolerated.

The white authorities were trying hard to create a rift between ANC and the people of South Africa. They were wooing both Buthelezi and the colored votes emphasizing over the voter ANC's anti-color stand. In July Nelson Mandela returned to South Africa after his political voyage to Uganda, Kenya ad Mozambique the request was forwarded to President Klerk about the violence and turmoil heighten up in the country. But the talks were again held back as the forty members of ANC were caught with a conspiracy to throw the government with the help of outsiders. Nelson Mandela claimed that he didn't know anything about the plot but de klerk wanted to keep ANC away and Joe Slovo the prime convict of operation valor from the talks. In September in a speech Mandela sensed that there was a third force consists of renegade men from the security forces who were disturbing the negotiations. On 22nd July Inkatha members with full bus loaded were escorted by police into their vehicles entered into a rally and attacked the gathering. The armed men rampaged murdering and hurting the people in the grisly attack. Nelson Mandela personally demanded explanation from President klerk but he kept mum.

In November Inkatha members entered a squatter's camp Zonkizizwe east of Johannesburg and drove ANC people out and subsequently killing some ANC workers. The Inkatha members were accompanying the police but once again President Mr. Klerk did not respond to this issue seriously or immediately. The government added fuel to the controversy by permitting Zulus to carry traditional weapons in rally. The weapons were used by Inkatha previously to kill ANC members. The government was using divide and rule tactics openly and immorally by secret funding to Inkatha and using it against ANC to weaken the force and trust it had with the masses.

ANC chose its leader

In July 1991 ANC held its first annual conference inside South Africa in thirty years which was attended by 2244 voting delegates and they democratically elected Nelson Mandela as the President of ANC without opposition. The ANC restored its unequivocal faith in Nelson Mandela once again. At the threshold of the most crucial phase in nations life, Nelson Mandela expressed his appreciation for the great honor bestowed upon him. He was bent down with proud but and conformed the responsibility. He was presided with "The point which must be clearly understood is that the struggle is not over and negotiations themselves are a threat of struggle subject to advances and reverses as any other form of struggle".(p-709)

Nelson Mandela understood the course of the tide and time. He realized that negotiations would not wait but it was not in their interest of the prolonged agony of apartheid for any reason. He urged all his fellow strugglers that a transitional governmental was the need of the hour.

Divorce from Winnie

Another weary of his personal as well as political life was his wife Winnie's involvement in suspicious and controversial episodes that followed with regular intervals. One of such incident happened as the kidnapping of four youths and the death of one of them. The case stood in the court and Winnie proven guilty. Her indirectly involvement in the crime proved her guilty and was punished with six years imprisonment. Though Nelson Mandela always kept his deep trust in judiciary commented personally that "her innocence was not in doubt." (P-711). But just after few months after showing his unattainable trust his wife Nelson Mandela in a joint press-conference on 13th April 1992 in Johannesburg with Walter and Oliver, announced his "separation from my wife".-(P-718). His separation was marked with his complete disregard for his wife's illegitimate and illegal deeds. "Circumstances beyond our control however dictated it should be otherwise". (P-719) His press conference with ANC comrades sent a strong message that it wasn't a personal matter anymore. It was a political decision and Nelson Mandela proved that at a time he would lose his personal stake for the political victory. He narrated the entire issue with lot of emotionality and sentimentally. He called it a political mistake of his wife and the mistake could not be forgiven if it was against the common goal. He showed his personal sacrifice for the party. He took the blame on himself and the circumstances but didn't speak against Winnie. "It seems to be the destiny of freedom figurers to have unstable personal lives." (P-719).

Throughout his auto-biography Winnie seemed to be with him in his struggle. She was pictured as supporting, caring and loving wife. He expressed very sentimental love towards her. Though she seemed to be lost her way. She did not follow the way of Nelson Mandela. He always stood by her and motivated her at each step. His narration, his words were dipped into most lovable feeling "I embrace her with all the love and affection I have nursed for her inside and outside prison from the moment I first met her."(P-719)

Negotiations

Nelson Mandela as a head of ANC was not only instrumental in power tactics but the guiding force behind the formation of convention for a democratic South Africa-CODESA. The first round of negotiations began between the Government and ANC that also included other parties. The widest cross-section of political group ever gathered at one place in South Africa for the future of the nation.

The sense of historical responsibility and the unity was exhibited by all the parties. The negotiations preceded without outside countries help like Zimbabwe and Angola. It was a moment of maturity and responsibility. Mr. de klerk talked about "Power sharing government on democratic basis. The National Party chief Dowie de villers offered an apology for apartheid." (P-713). And Nelson Mandela promisingly admired, CODESA marked "the beginning of the road to an elected assembly that would write a new constitution." (P-713).

CODESA-I- Nelson Mandela viewed it as the first step in a process to establish an independent judiciary. Protection of civil liberties, multi-party democracy and common voter's rights were the main suggestions came up in the discussion. With his efforts certainly reported to give each one his own stake of power and justice.

CODESA- New battle ground

But CODESA became a battle ground of egoism, self-centeredness and doubtfulness. Mr. de Klerk and other party members started the feeling sonority because Nelson Mandela's seemed to be growing in status with his hold on the discussion. Mr. de Klerk asked for a favor from him to allow him to give concluding speech on the first day of CODESA. Nelson Mandela and his party permitted him by persuading other party members. But Mr. de klarke misused that opportunity against ANC by attacking the ANC for not adhering to the agreements made with the governments and berated ANC for failing to disclose the location of arms canes and rebuked for maintaining "private army" Umkhouto we sizwe.

That was intolerable and false blame on ANC. Nelson Mandela came heavily and severely attacked Mr. De Klark as "illegitimate discredited minority regime"(P-715). He reiterated that it was ANC who made up the talks and it was the government who failed the talks. He admitted that ANC would return the arms only when they would be the part of the government and contemned the government for funding organization that were committed violence against ANC. Next day both Nelson Mandela and Mr. De Klarke came together and shook hands. They took pains to show that no irreparable harm had been done but he found that much trust had been lost and the negations were in the slate of disarray.

Mr. De Klerk played a gamble to match himself with Nelson Mandela by proving that he also enjoyed the same support and appreciation among white alike his rival among Black. A referendum was called for vote on the issue of his reform policy and on negotiations with the ANC. He stated that if he was defeated he would resign. Mr. de klerk's campaign got remarkable success 69 percentage of white voters supported negotiations. But Nelson Mandela found it "dangerous strategy."(P-717)

In May 1992 second round of talks CODESA-2 began on the scandalous setbacks to the government. First was the revelation of massive corruption and bribery in Government and the second was the murder of four of UDF members. These were the tragedies Nelson Mandela accounted them as undermining government's morality and strengthening their hands.

CODESA ultimately broke down on four issues- The Governments' non- acceptance on higher percentage votes subsequently during majority regional powers autonomy, the unelected senate in the power structure and the supreme power ' veto power over legislation' given to non-elected senate and no to the determination to make a permanent constitution.

4th August – Nationwide Strike

On the backdrop of these negotiations progress, an unfortunate event happened that widen the rift between Government and

ANC. 17th June 1992 known in South Africa as a mournful memory of "Sharpeville" massacre, on the day a heavily armed force of Inkatha secretly raided Vaal township of Biopatong killing forty-six people. Mr. de Klarke said nothing as usual.

Nelson Mandela addressed a crowd of twenty thousand angry supporters but instead of fueling the violent crowd, he suggested a non-violent Gandhian way of protest. The crowd was carrying the sign of "Mandela Give us weapon" "Victory Through Battle Not talks".

Nelson Mandela realized that "it was a time to cool."(P-724) The anger and emotions of the people were intense. To give way to it in positive way, Nelson Mandela proposed nationwide strike on 4th August for ANC's negotiation demand and protest against state sponsored violence. The mass action campaign was the largest political strike in South African history. More than 4 million people stayed at home and a march of one hundred thousand protesters on Government Building.

The violence continued on 7th September in Bisho stadium. The homeland troop gunned down 29 peaceful protester and wounded two hundred. In another incident Mr. Chris Haui the general secretory of SABC and former MK chief was shot dead. Nelson Mandela spoke on SABC and calmed the violent people--- "Now is the time for all South Africans Black and White to stand together against those who from any quarter wish to destroy what Chris Haui gave his life for the freedom of all of us"(P-730).

Nobel Award

3rd June 1993 was the landmark day in South African history. The multiparty forum voted to set a date 27th April 1994 a date for the country's first national non-racial one person one vote election. This peace talks and democratic efforts between Nelson Mandela and President de Klerk were appreciated by world peace makers. The highest award Noble peace prize was declared in 1993 to Nelson Mandela and President Klerk jointly. He was the third African to be honored with this prestigious international award. "The award was a tribute to all South Africans and especially to those who had fought in the struggle" (P-735) Nelson Mandela thanked the committee with gratitude and respect. He also reported his surprise that he was accused of violence and yet Nobel committee considered him for the prize. The prize was the answer to all the criticizers who condemned him in the past for violence. He went to accept the award jointly with President Klerk a symbolic gesture of unity and reconciliation. But the act was condemned by few who did not like Nelson Mandela to join hands with those who were the enemies of blacks and cause of their bloodshed for centuries.

Mr. de klerk had been a prime abuser of ANC and had been poised for sponsoring brutal attacks on ANC members but Nelson Mandela accepted the award for his role as the "indispensable contributor in the peace process" and it was the most humanitarian gesture as he became true ambassador of peace and peace maker. In his own words, "To make a peace with the enemy one must work with the enemy and that enemy become your partner."(P-735).

Voting and Victory

3rd June 1993 was the landmark day in South African history. The multiparty forum voted to set a date 27th April 1994 a date for the country's first national non-racial one person one vote election. Voting day was not only special and historical for South Africa but also very nostalgic and filled with the gratification memories for Nelson Mandela. He deliberately choose Ohlange school of Inada to cast his vote. The historically nostalgic place he selected because it was the place where the first president of ANC John Dade was buried in 1912. His mind dwelt on the memories of heroes who had fallen so that South-Africa could see this day. Oliver Tamboo, Chris Haui, Chief Luthuli, Bram fisher of the past and many others of the present day he recalled on this special historical day.

Despite the efforts of the Government to split the votes into different smaller parties and the negative propaganda by other smaller parties against ANC and Nelson Mandela, the democratic elections proved that Nelson Mandela and ANC were the most popular in South Africa. Two third land slide victory was achieved by Nelson Mandela and ANC. It was the stamp of Nelson Mandela's popularity, integrity and ANC's hard efforts against apartheid.

On 10 May 1994, Nelson Mandela took the pledge to obey and uphold the constitution – in his memorable speech he spoke, " Out of the experience of an extra ordinary human disaster that lasted too long, must be born a society of which all humanity will be proud-----The sun shall never set on so glorious a human achievement." (P-747).

Conclusion

The autobiography concludes with an ordinary boy from tribal village Qunu becoming the first black President of democratic South Africa. Nelson Mandela became the face for fortitude, resilience and highest sacrifice. He helped the country through his political party African National Congress to achieve miracle that no South African believed. Apartheid was the cruelest political system existed till the end of 2oth century. The apartheid system propagated racism, injustice and inequality. The system existed for nearly 400 years in South Africa. It was always difficult to end an old, outdated and colonial system. American, French, Russian revolutions and all independence struggles against colonialism were the examples of victory of masses over the minority rulers who ruled for their benefit and selfishness. The victory of South Africa though came very late celebrated the faith and victory of humanism over anarchy of few.

References:

1) (https://www.whitehouse.gov/the-press-office/2013/12/10/remarks-president-obama-memorial-service-former-south-african-president-)
2) (http://www.theguardian.com/world/2014/jul/14/nadine-gordimer-nelson-mandela-your-favourite-protest-writers)
3) https://www.nelsonmandela.org/news/entry/nelson-mandela-foundation-sends-condolences-on-the-passing-of-nadine-gordimer
4) http://www.latimes.com/opinion/op-ed/la-oe-atuahene-mandela-land-south-africa-20141207-story.html)
5) http://www.aucegypt.edu/gapp/cairoreview/pages/article details.aspx?aid=69
6) Edward Said, *Humanism and Democratic Criticism* (New York: Columbia University Press, 2004), p. 26.

7) *Bell brooks,* Killing Rage Ending Racism (London: Penguin Books, 1995), p. 241.

8) Mary Benson, *Nelson Mandela: the Man and the Movement* (London: W. W. Norton & Company, 994), p. 2.
9) Benson, *Nelson Mandela: the Man and the Movement*, p. 3.

10) *Tim Juckes, Opposition in South Africa* the leadership of Z.K. Matthews, Nelson Mandela, and Stephen Biko *(Westport: Praeger, 1995), p. 83.*

11) Juckes, Opposition in South Africa *the leadership of Z.K. Matthews, Nelson Mandela, and Stephen Biko*, p. 314

12) W. J. T. Mitchell, *Picture Theory: Essays on Verbal and Visual Representation* (Chicago: University of Chicago Press, 1995), p. 312.

13) Mitchell, *Picture Theory: Essays on Verbal and Visual Representation*, p. 315.

14) Gallagher, Susan VanZanten, *A Story of South Africa: J. M. Coetzee's Fiction in Context* (Cambridge: Harvard University Press, 1991), p. 156.

15) Abdul R. JanMohamed, 'The Economy of Manichean Allegory: The Function of Racial Difference in Colonialist Literature', *Race, Writing and Difference*, Edited by Henry Louis Gates (Chicago: University of Chicago Press, 1986), p. 80.

ABOUT THE AUTHOR

Dr. Nandkumar S Shinde
M.A. (SET) PhD
English
Assistant Professor
Symbiosis Skills and Open University
Pune.

Printed in Great Britain
by Amazon

11352957R10066